"ALL OVER BY CHRISTMAS..."

David Berguer

148 Friern Park
London
N12 9LU
First published 2014

© David Berguer

The right of David Berguer to be identified as the Author of this work has been asserted in accordance with the Copyrights, Designs and Patents Act 1988.

All rights reserved. No part of this book may be reprinted or reproduced or utilised in any form or by any electronic, mechanical or other means now known or hereafter invented including photocopying or recording, or in any information storage or retrieval system, without the permission in writing from the Publisher, nor otherwise be circulated in any form of binding or cover other than that in which it is published without similar condition including this condition being imposed on the subsequent purchaser.

A catalogue entry is available from the British Library

ISBN 9 780956 934499

Front cover images courtesy of Imperial War Museum
(left to right, top to bottom (©IWM PST 10063), (©IWM PST Q33161), (©IWM PST 12052), (©Q71311), (©IWM PST 5996)

Front and back cover design by DesignbyCaroline.co.uk
Printed and bound in Great Britain by Jellyfish Print Solutions

Also by David Berguer:

"The Friern Hospital Story: The history of a Victorian Lunatic Asylum"
ISBN 9 780956 934444

"Under the Wires at Tally Ho: Trams and Trolleybuses of North London 1905-1962" ISBN 9 780752 48755

CONTENTS

INTRODUCTION			4
CHAPTER 1	HOW IT ALL STARTED		6
CHAPTER 2	THE EARLY DAYS		12
CHAPTER 3	PROPAGANDA		27
CHAPTER 4	LETTERS FROM THE FRONT		38
CHAPTER 5	LETTERS FROM HOME		58
CHAPTER 6	SEND MORE MEN		83
CHAPTER 7	THE COST OF THE WAR		99
CHAPTER 8	FEEDING THE FAMILY		104
CHAPTER 9	RESTRICTIONS AT HOME		126
CHAPTER 10	THE DEMON DRINK		134
CHAPTER 11	WOMEN AT WAR		140
CHAPTER 12	FOUR MEN'S WAR		160
CHAPTER 13	TERROR FROM THE AIR		171
CHAPTER 14	THE END		192
CHAPTER 15	THE LEGACY		203
CHAPTER 16	MEMORIALS		212
INDEX			220
APPENDIX A	CHRONOLOGY: THE HOME FRONT		227
APPENDIX B	CHRONONLOGY: THE WESTERN FRONT		234
APPENDIX C	THE WAR DEAD		243
APPENDIX D	ZEPPELIN RAIDS ON BRITAIN		265
APPENDIX E	AEROPLANE RAIDS ON BRITAIN		270
APPENDIX F	PENSIONS FOR THE WAR DISABLED		275

INTRODUCTION

The idea for this book came from John Heathfield, President of the Friern Barnet & District Local History Society, who suggested to the committee that we should do something to mark the centenary of the outbreak of the First World War. Initially it was envisaged that this would be a ten or twelve page publication, in the style of a number of *Brief Histories* which the Society has published before, but the fact that it has ended up much larger is down largely to the sterling work done by Nick McKie, Treasurer of the Society. Nick decided to look at the local newspapers of the period and he spent many hours at the Newspaper Library at Colindale studying microfilm copies of the *Barnet Press* and then printing off relevant articles.

It soon became clear that this was an excellent source. We had no idea that he would uncover letters from the Front conveying in amazing detail the horrors of the trenches and the conditions of the troops. There was so much material that it became a question of not what to include, but what to leave out. With this wealth of material it was decided that the work should be expanded to try and give a flavour of what everyday life was like in Finchley, Friern Barnet, New Southgate, North Finchley and Whetstone and in London in general.

An even more intriguing source was provided by Anthea Gray who had a collection of over 200 letters that her mother had written to her father during the war when he was stationed in Egypt, at some time working alongside T E Lawrence. These letters gave a great insight into the events on the Home Front and her mother's reactions to them. I am indebted to Anthea for allowing me to publish extracts from these.

Minute books of the Friern Barnet Urban District Council and Finchley Council were another source of material and thanks are due to Hugh Petrie of Barnet Local Studies and Archives for his help in the project.

Another excellent source of material was provided by local historian Percy Reboul who some twenty years ago had interviewed several people who had memories of the war and his tapes of these interviews have proved invaluable. Percy also had a collection of magazines of the period which he very kindly lent me and from which I have extracted a number of advertisements which help to make the past spring to life.

A special thanks to my wife, Patricia, and members of the Friern Barnet & District Local History Society for their support and encouragement and for checking the drafts and pointing out errors.

There have been hundreds of books, films and television programmes on the First World War and it would be pointless to try and go over old ground, so I have made no attempt to describe the battles that took place, but there is a chronology giving details of the battles on the Western Front.

Thanks to the diligent work of John Heathfield and John Philpott I am able to include a list of some of the war dead in the Friern Barnet area which have been recorded on gravestones and memorials, together with, in some cases, brief details of their circumstances where these are known. Hopefully these may be of use to future historians or to those researching family history.

Every effort has been made to trace copyright holders; those overlooked are invited to get in touch with the publishers.

I hope that this book will prove of interest to the general reader and maybe in 2039 a similar work will be produced to mark the outbreak of the Second World War which took place twenty five years after the outbreak of "the war to end all wars."

David Berguer
Chairman
Friern Barnet & District Local History Society

CHAPTER 1

HOW IT ALL STARTED

The exact cause of the war is a matter of some controversy among modern day historians and there is no doubt that it is virtually impossible to attribute one single reason.

Before 1914 Europe was dominated by five great powers: Britain with its vast empire and powerful navy; France; the newly created Germany; Austria-Hungary (the Habsburg Empire) and Russia. Each of the powers had undergone recent problems which made them feel insecure.

In 1870 France had gone to war with Prussia (the Franco-Prussian war) which she lost and had been forced to surrender the mainly German-speaking territories of Alsace and Lorraine to Prussia.

The new country of Germany had been created in 1871 from 39 separate states by the Prussian Chancellor, Otto von Bismarck (the Iron Chancellor) and Wilhelm was declared the first Kaiser. When in 1899 Britain had got involved in the Boer War Germany had shown sympathy to the Boers to the extent that they considered helping them. By 1914 Germany had become the largest military organisation in the world and the second most powerful. Germany was also a major industrial nation. In 1913 Britain's exports to Germany were £40,700,000 (mainly raw materials) whereas German exports to Britain were nearly double that - £80,400,000, mainly manufactured goods.

Emperor Franz Ferdinand was head of Austria-Hungary, an alliance of two racially different cultures of whom half were Slavs.

Russia was led by the weak Nicholas II who was under the influence of his German wife and the evil monk Rasputin. In 1904 Nicholas had declared war on Japan but was humiliatingly defeated and that led the following year to civil unrest in Russia; this was ruthlessly crushed but would eventually mean revolution and the creation of a communist state in 1917.

There was one particular flashpoint in Europe at the time – the Balkans (Serbia, Bulgaria and Romania) which had until recently been part of the Turkish Ottoman Empire and which now wanted to run their own affairs. However, both Austria-Hungary and Russia had common borders with the Balkan states and each tried to exert their influence on them, the Russians in particular because of their common Slavic heritage. The Germans backed Austria-Hungary.

Because of these feelings of insecurity at the time, countries had formed various alliances and it was these that would eventually lead to the outbreak of the First World War.

In 1879 Germany had formed a Dual Alliance with Austria-Hungary under which they would help each other if attacked. This became a Triple Alliance when Italy joined.

In 1893 France and Russia had become allies and this caused disquiet in Germany which considered itself under threat from both its western and eastern borders.

An Anglo-French accord was reached in 1904 (the *Entente Cordiale*). It was not an alliance as such, but an agreement to work closer together. Russia then joined and it became a Triple Entente and led to Germany now feeling even more threatened. To counter a threat from France and Russia, Germany had in 1905 drawn up a plan of action (the Schlieffen Plan) whereby France would be invaded first with a massive force and, once this had been achieved, a second front would be opened against Russia.

Things came to a head in Europe when the heir to the throne of Austria-Hungary, Archduke Franz Ferdinand, and his wife Sophie were visiting Sarajevo in Bosnia in the summer of 1914. On Sunday 28 June they were driving in an open topped car through Sarajevo; he was dressed in a sky-blue tunic with a helmet of green peacock feathers and she was attired in white silk. A young Serb nationalist, Gavrilo Princip, broke through the crowd surrounding Franz Ferdinand's car and fired two shots, killing both of them. He was arrested and later tried but because of his age, he escaped being executed and later died in prison.

On 23 July Austria-Hungary issued a series of political demands to Serbia which they knew would be unacceptable to the Serbs. Having received no positive response, on 28 July Austria-Hungary declared war on Serbia. This triggered off a rapidly moving series of events that would plunge Europe and the world, into war.

Britain had asked both France and Germany to respect the neutrality of Belgium. The ultimatum to Germany was delivered by Sir Edward Goschen, the British Ambassador in Berlin, and read:

> "Sir Edward Goschen has been informed by Sir Edward Grey that His Majesty the King of the Belgians has addressed to His Majesty King George an appeal for diplomatic intervention on behalf of Belgium.
>
> His Majesty's Government are also informed that a note has been delivered to the Belgian Government by the German Government proposing friendly neutrality entailing free passage through Belgian territory and promising to maintain at the conclusion of peace the independence and integrity of the Kingdom and its possessions, threatening to treat Belgium as an enemy in case of refusal. It was requested that an answer might be retuned within twelve hours.
>
> His Majesty's Government also understand that this request has been categorically refused by Belgium as a flagrant violation of the Law of Nations.
>
> Sir Edward Grey states that His Majesty's Government are bound to protest against this violation of a Treaty to which Germany is a party in common with themselves and that they must request an assurance that the demand made upon Belgium will not be proceeded with and that Germany will respect the neutrality of Belgium.
>
> Sir Edward Goschen is instructed to ask for an immediate reply.
>
> BERLIN, August 4, 1914."

France agreed to respect Belgium's neutrality but Germany did not even bother to reply. On 1 August Germany declared war on Russia and two days later declared war on France. At 11 o'clock in the evening of Tuesday 4 August (midnight in Berlin) Britain's ultimatum expired and consequently Britain declared war on Germany which, in accordance with the Schlieffen Plan, then started to move troops through Belgium, entering France on 24

August. Britain in turn sent an Expeditionary Force of around 80,000 men to France.

On 6 August Austria-Hungary declared war on Russia and on 10 August both Britain and France declared war on Austria-Hungary. On 1 November Russia declared war on the Turkish Ottoman Empire, and its allies did likewise on 5 November. In 1915 more countries entered the fray:

- On 15 March Austria-Hungary declared war on Portugal,
- On 23 May Italy declared war on Austria-Hungary
- On 20 August Italy declared war on Turkey
- On 12 October Bulgaria declared war on Serbia
- On 14 October France and Britain declared war on Bulgaria.
- On 1 November Russia declared war on Turkey

The following year more countries got involved:

- On 15 March 1916 Austria-Hungary declares war on Portugal
- On 27 August Romania declares war on Austria-Hungary
- On 28 August Germany declared war on Romania
- On 30 August Turkey declared war on Romania
- On 1 September Bulgaria declared war on Romania
- On 27 November Greece declared war on Germany.

A complication was the relationship between the various European royal families. Tsar Nicholas II and Kaiser Wilhelm II were cousins while George V was first cousin of Nicholas on one side of the family and of

Wilhelm on the other. George was also related to both their wives. The Kaiser was an honorary admiral of the British fleet, a position he relinquished after war was declared and in May 1915 King George V stripped Wilhelm of the Order of the Garter. On 17 July 1917 the House of Windsor was created which apparently prompted Kaiser Wilhelm to say that he was going to the theatre to see *The Merry Wives of Saxe-Coburg-Gotha*. At the same time Battenberg became Mountbatten.

The Foreign Secretary, Sir Edward Grey, is credited with making the most quoted comment on the situation in 1914 when, speaking to a friend, he said: "The lamps are going out all over Europe; we shall not see them lit again in our time."

CHAPTER 2

THE EARLY DAYS

When news reached Britain of the assassination of a member of a minor royal family in a place most people had never even heard of, it sparked little interest and in the hot summer of 1914 the general feeling in Britain was "it will all be over by Christmas" and people got on with their daily lives. Their attention was also focussed much nearer home where the rise of Irish nationalism and the demand for home rule was threatening a civil war in Ireland. History had also shown that many of the conflicts in Europe in the 19th century had been low-level affairs that often lasted months rather than years; Britain had last fought a war on European soil nearly a hundred years previously at the Battle of Waterloo in 1815. The feeling that this was only going to be a short war was echoed in Germany where the Kaiser told German troops: "You will be returning home before the leaves have fallen from the trees."

However, once war had been declared the harsh reality began to dawn. The *Barnet Press* carried articles publicising various public meetings.

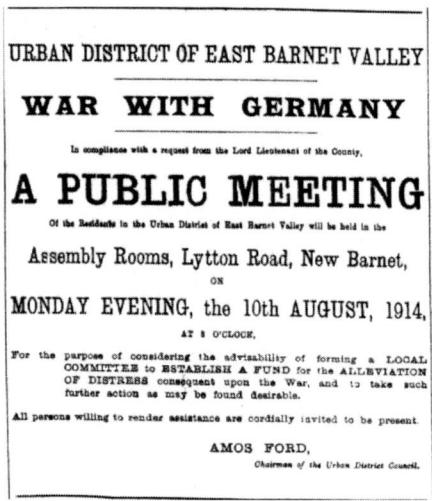

A War Distress Meeting was held in Whetstone to appoint a local committee 'to relieve distress in the district during the war'. The meeting, which was packed and included many ladies, considered two points, firstly how to raise the necessary funds and secondly how they should be distributed.

Field-Marshal Lord Kitchener, the Secretary of State for War, asked Parliament on 6 August 1914 to authorise the recruitment of 500,000 soldiers to supplement the regular army of 257,000 men, most of whom were posted abroad in the British Empire. In addition to this, there was a reserve army of Territorials amounted to 620,000, but these were not meant to fight abroad. To put these figures into context, the German army at the time numbered 1.5 million.

The initial appeal was for 100,000 but such was the response that this was soon achieved and a call for a further 100,000 men was made on 28 August, the age limit was raised from 30 to 35 and an appeal was made to married men in particular. By 15 September the target had been reached, with volunteers flocking to the recruiting stations which were unable to cope.

(©IWMQ48378a)
Lord Kitchener's famous appeal to the country

> **YOUR COUNTRY NEED YOU**
> **A CALL TO ARMS**
>
> An addition of 100,000 men to His Majesty's Regular Army is immediately necessary in the present grave National Emergency. Lord Kitchener is confident that this appeal will be at once responded top by all who have the safety of our Empire at heart.
>
> **TERMS OF SERVICE**
> General service for a period of three years, or until the War is concluded.
>
> Age of enlistment, between 19 and 30

Although enlistment was not a problem, supplying the recruits proved a logistical nightmare as there was a shortage of equipment and uniforms for them and buildings to house them in. Tented camps had to be set up throughout the country and buildings requisitioned until things could be better organised.

Lord Kitchener's decision to set the period of service at 'three years, or until the war is concluded' proved to be strangely prophetic, although few signing up at the time could have anticipated that the war would last longer than a few months.

Crowds outside a recruiting office

New recruits take the Oath of Allegiance

TERRITORIAL FORCE.

MIDDLESEX (RESERVE) BRIGADE COMPANY ARMY SERVICE CORPS.

RECRUITS
MAY NOW JOIN THIS NEW UNIT.

Men accustomed to Riding and Driving and the management of horses are especially required. Wheelwrights, Saddlers, and Farriers for the Mounted Section, and Clerks, Butchers, and Bakers for the Dismounted Section.

Pay at Army Rates, and Separation Allowance for Married Men, will be granted from date of Enlistment.

ALL RECRUITS TO SIGN FOR FOREIGN SERVICE, AND WILL BE ALLOWED TO CLAIM THEIR DISCHARGES AT THE END OF THE WAR.

Full particulars can be obtained any time from
CORPORAL BOSSOM, The Barracks, Barnet.

September, 1914.   J. H. DRESSER, Major.

"GOD SAVE THE KING."

(Barnet Press 26 Sep 1914)

Territorials marching over Westminster Bridge

An article in the August 1914 issue of *All Saints' Parish Magazine Friern Barnet* summed up the initial feelings:

> "How little we thought when our last Magazine was issued what tragedies were before us. For years, there have been rumours of the danger of a European war, but we have always felt that the very awfulness of it under modern conditions would be the greatest safeguard against it, and that the nations of Europe would vie with one another in their endeavours to prevent, by the science of diplomacy, such an awful outrage upon our civilization and our Christianity. So we hoped up to the last moment of possibility, and then in a few days our hopes were utterly shattered, and we found ourselves forced into the appalling catastrophe which we had

believed to be impossible. We could not for a moment entertain the "infamous proposal" made to us by Germany, nor could we ever have lifted up our head again as a nation if we had allowed a treaty to be broken or a small nation to be crushed. The Government stood firm; all parties were united in supporting them and those who had laboured most for peace were of one mind in upholding the declaration of war; the whole country has approved the action of those in authority; contending parties are united in the common cause; breaches which seemed to be hopeless have been closed and healed; thousands have come forward to help in various ways, and the United Kingdom has been more truly united than it has been for many years. We are most thankful that in our own Parish many of our young men have offered themselves in their country's cause, and many others have shown themselves ready to make such sacrifices and to do such work as seem to be required of them."

At that time in Britain's history pride in the country and the patriotism that people felt, coupled with feelings of hope and faith, were much stronger than they are today and strong feelings for 'our brave lads' at the front and their love of the girls they had left behind were responsible for the initial rush to enlist. A speech given by David Lloyd George, then the Chancellor of the Exchequer, on 15 September 1914 summed up the general feelings:

"There is no man in this room who has always regarded the prospect of engaging in a great war with greater reluctance than I have done through the whole period of my political life. There is no man inside or outside this room more convinced that we could not have avoided it without national dishonour…they think we cannot beat them. It will not be easy. It will be a long job. It will be a terrible war. But in the end we will march through terror to triumph. We shall need all our qualities – every quality that Britain and its people possess – prudence in counsel, daring in action, tenacity in purpose, courage in defeat, moderation in victory, in all things faith."

On 8 August 1914 the Defence of the Realm Act (DORA) was passed. The Act itself was surprisingly short in length but wide-ranging in the powers it gave:

> "An Act to confer on His Majesty in Council power to make Regulations during the present War for the Defence of the Realm.
>
> Be it enacted by the King's most excellent majesty by and with the advice and consent of the Lords Spiritual and Temporal, and Commons, in this present Parliament assembled, and by the authority of the same, as follows:
>
> 1. His Majesty in Council has power during the continuance of the present war to issue regulations as to the powers and duties of the Admiralty and Army Council, and of the members of His Majesty's forces, and other persons acting on his behalf, for securing the public safety and the defence of the realm; and may by such regulations authorize the trial by courts martial and punishment of persons contravening any of the provisions of such regulations designed:
>   (a) to prevent persons communicating with the enemy or obtaining information for that purpose or any purpose calculated to jeopardise the success of the operations of any of His Majesty's forces or to assist the enemy, or:
>   (b) to secure the safety of any means of communication, or of railways, docks or harbours;
>
> in a like manner as if such persons were subject to military law and had on active service committed an offence under section five of the Army Act."

The powers ranged from the requisitioning of buildings or land to the creation of a number of new criminal offences such as the flying of kites (which, it was feared, could attract Zeppelins). The demand for horses to ferry supplies to the Front from depots behind the lines and to haul heavy guns led to the requisitioning of many of them from private owners and farmers in particular. Additions were made to the Act as the war progressed, in particular the Consolidation Act of 27 November 1914 which authorised the death penalty for cases of 'offences committed with the intention of assisting the enemy.' Civil liberties were thus drastically reduced and civilians charged with violations of the Act could be tried by a military court martial, with serious violations carrying the death penalty.

There were some 50,000 Germans working in Britain at the time and, not surprisingly, they were singled out in the early days. In North Finchley on Friday 2 August 1914 a mob attacked the premises of Mr H Flack, a Russian Jew, in Park Parade. Using bricks from the site of the new Jelks' furniture store which was under construction, they practically demolished the premises. Apparently Mr Flack was alleged to have made anti-British remarks 'likely to cause a breach of the peace.' Inspector Wallis and a group of constables arrived by tram which had driven non-stop from Finchley police station, much to the consternation of the passengers, some of whom were carried past their stop. They (the police, not the passengers) charged the mob and dispersed it. The *Barnet Press* reported that the 'crowd were not out for plunder, as was shown by the fact that, when boxes of chocolates fell through the broken windows on to the pavement, the only chocolate snatcher was a dog which showed praiseworthy discrimination in sorting out the confectionery from the pieces of broken glass.'

Charles Cooper, 31, and James Butcher were charged with damaging Mr Flack's windows, the damage amounting to £60 or £70. The Chairman of the Bench said: "This is not the sort of behaviour we expect of an Englishman though no doubt it is common in other countries." Frederick Cox and his wife Thelma were charged with disorderly conduct. Sergeant Floyd said there was a crowd of about 800 and he asked the accused to move on and she knocked his helmet off. Cox said: "I can stand here as long as I like." John Cox of Grove Road was charged with trying to rescue the couple and PC210 said in his evidence that he had asked him to go away to which Cox replied: "Fifty policemen will not make me." The three were fined five shillings each. A Mrs Mardin of East Finchley was charged with insulting behaviour – she had abused her neighbour Mrs Mary Dick. In her defence she said she thought Mrs Dick was German. She was bound over to keep the peace.

An East Finchley hairdresser with a German sounding name took the precaution of having this removed from the shop and replacing it with 'East Finchley Hairdressing Salon' and another East Finchley shopkeeper renamed his shop 'Market-parade Bakery'. A Mr Ritsert from North Finchley, a naturalised Englishman flew a Union Jack from his upper windows which 'afforded him ample protection.'

Anti-German feeling was aroused again the following year. On 1 May 1915 the British liner *RMS Lusitania* left New York for Liverpool and the German government issued the following notice in American newspapers:

> "Travellers intending to embark on the Atlantic voyage are reminded that a state of war exists between Germany and her allies and Great Britain and her allies; that the zone of war includes the waters adjacent to the British Isles; that, in accordance with formal notice given by the Imperial German Government, vessels flying the flag of Great Britain, or any of her allies, are liable to destruction in those waters and that travellers sailing in the war zone on the ships of Great Britain or her allies do so at their own risk
>
> IMPERIAL GERMAN EMBASSY
>
> Washington, D.C., April 22, 1915"

On 7 May the *Lusitania* was torpedoed by a German submarine off the Irish coast and she sank with the loss of 1195 lives. There was outrage both in Britain and America (there were 139 US citizens on board) and feelings ran high as the *Barnet Press* reported on 22 May 1915:

> "'Remember the Lusitania.' This was the cry of a crowd of New Southgate citizens who paraded the street last weekend looking for aliens. They did but little damage. Three windows were broken, one

> belonging to a man in the High-street, one belonging to a man in the Station-road, and one belonging to a man on the Freehold. What could have happened but for the presence of a large force of special constables we fear to say. The crowd demonstrated their indignation in all sorts of peculiar ways. One man whistled the "Marseillaise" through the keyhole of a German's front door; another gave an Irish clog dance on a German's doorstep to the tune of the Belgian National Anthem. A great raid was arranged to take place on Thursday night, but the ardour of the raiders cooled under a deluge of rain, and at the time appointed for the commencement of proceedings most of the raiders were in bed sound asleep."

Another view of the outrage felt was written by Mabel Holman, writing to her fiancée in Egypt on 16 May 1915:

> "The terrible news of the sinking of the "Lusitania" and loss of 1500 lives – murder verdict against the Kaiser. I spent an anxious night as Henry Bentley had cabled he was leaving America immediately per "Lusitania" and of course we all thought he was on it, but in the morning we received a cable to say he had missed the boat which was providence if you like. On Monday lunch time I found Cullum Street in turmoil and found a huge crowd had insisted on the shutting of 3 shops – a German restaurant, provision shop and chemists. This was done by City gentlemen and everyone's blood is up. This went on every day - meetings have been held all over the City. They are all turned out of the Stock Exchange, Baltic and other large places and everyone with a foreign name is chased or made to shut up shop. Of course things got from bad to worse as the east end started and there have been terrible goings on. I narrowly escaped a stone in my eye one day. Things got to such a pitch that the Govt. at last has ordered the internment of all aliens – so I should think. Lots of places will not even serve Germans – I loathe the sight of any foreigners now. ….I don't think there is a bakers shop in the country without its windows smashed."

As the war progressed and reports of conditions at the Front began to appear, public attitude began to change. In April 1915 the Friern Barnet Relief Fund had received 256 applications from wives and dependents of soldiers, and they were able to offer assistance in 235 of the cases. By August of the same year the fund stood at £1090 and payments totalled £857. Help was also given to 95 people made unemployed by the war; of these, 39 received help from the fund, 40 were offered employed by Friern Barnet UDC and 13 were referred to the Poor Law. In January 1917 *All Saints' Parish Magazine* reported:

> "The all Saints' and St James' War Savings Association has been working for 22 weeks during which time over 430 certificates have been bought, of which 400 have been fully paid up and allocated to members. A total sum of nearly £350 has been lent thereby to the nation. Our membership has increased from 24 (enrolled on the first day) to 176. February 12th to 19th was "War Savings Week" when every scholar from the tiniest infant to the biggest boy made every effort to obtain new members and more money. Such a week has never been known before. Sixty-two new members have been enrolled, and excitement rose to fever pitch when we found that the object of our aims was likely to be realized, viz., £100 during the week! Now, thanking all our subscribers for giving our children the happiness of knowing that they, too, are useful citizens of our dear old Country, we gladly announce that our takings are for the entire week £128 15s 0d. Hurrah for the children!"

A local man, John Parr, was the first British soldier to be killed in the First World War.

John was born in 1898 and lived at 52 Lodge Lane. His father, Edward (Teddy), worked as a milkman for United Dairies in Fredericks Place, off the High Road, North Finchley. He would have gone to Finchley Board School in Albert Street. His academic record might best be described as undistinguished and like others at the time he left school at 14 and got a job as a caddy at North Middlesex Golf Club.

1914 was a bad time for a poorly educated, unskilled working class lad. Jobs were scarce and he would have been looking for somewhere which provided accommodation, food and clothing. He joined the Army at Mill Hill Barracks, home of the 4th Battalion of the Middlesex Regiment, almost certainly lying about his age. Unfortunately his attestation certificate has disappeared.

In August 1914 the battalion was at Devonport, part of 8 Brigade, 3rd Division. The battalion entrained for Southampton and sailed in the *SS Mombassa* to Boulogne. On 22 August they moved up to the line of the Mons-Conde canal, which they used as a defence line. The first British shots in the war were fired by D company to which Private Parr was attached. They fired on a detachment of Uhlans – German cavalry wearing the typical flat topped caps and armed with lances. John Parr was part of the reconnaissance platoon and was sent towards Obourg to locate the enemy. There were shots fired and Private Parr failed to return. In the confusion which followed, the outnumbered British retreated towards Mons and subsequently to Nouvelles, Nine officers were killed and six wounded. A total of 453 other ranks were reported killed as killed, wounded or missing. Gradually about 200 men who had been separated re-joined the battalion. The confusion was such that the regimental war diary was not written until 3 days later.

At that period British soldiers did not wear dog tags and so John Parr's body was not formally identified until March 1915. Letters to the War Office from his frantic mother were unanswered because nobody knew what had happened.

"Sir,

I have been to the War Office today, October 26, concerning my son Private John Parr 14196D Company, 4th Battalion Middlesex 8th Infantry, who went on active service in August. I have not heard from him at all and the War Office seems to think that it is a rather long time. I am very anxious as it is now ten weeks. If anything has happened to him by this time, someone would have wrote *(sic)* to me.

I have heard from Berlin, the address is from a prisoner of war, one of my son's chums to say that my son.was shot down at Mons (a friend of John's, who had been captured, wrote from Germany to say John had been killed at Mons). I went to the War Office, they know nothing. An early reply will oblige.

Yours truly,

Mrs Parr"

It is possible that when the War Office realised that an under-age boy had been killed, the papers were "mislaid." Eventually news of Parr's fate came through the Swiss Red Cross. John Parr is buried at St Symphorien cemetery, just south of Mons.

The First World War was unique in that it was the first conflict to feature on the one hand the traditional aspects of warfare – large cavalry regiments mounted on horses and armed with swords, and artillery regiments who still practised with bayonets, and on the other hand the use of modern inventions – aeroplanes, radios, tanks and poison gas. When war broke out, French soldiers were still equipped with their traditional uniforms of bright blue tunics and red trousers while the cavalry were attired with brass helmets with long plumes, all which made them easy targets for German machine gunners. The failure of the military leaders to fully realise the potential of the new weapons at their disposal is shown by their initial reluctance to use the capability of aeroplanes to offer aerial photographs of the battlefield and, unbelievably, when tanks were first introduced in September 1916 they were not equipped with radios, relying instead in homing pigeons which were kept on board.

John Parr's grave at St Symphorien
(photo Percy Reboul)

TANKS!

Official Pictures of the British Army in France.

ADVANCE OF THE TANKS

On MONDAY NEXT, and every day at 3, 5, 7, and 9 o'clock throughout the week, at the

GRAND HALL,

NORTH FINCHLEY (Tally Ho Corner).

Augmented Orchestra.   Prices as usual.   Descriptive Programme, price 2d.
Seats may be booked.

('Barnet Press' 13 January 1917)

FINCHLEY RINK CINEMA,

HIGH ROAD, NORTH FINCHLEY, N.   Telephone FINCHLEY 1611

For Three Days, commencing MONDAY, JANUARY 15th:

"THE WHEELS OF JUSTICE,"
A Vitagraph "Blue Ribbon" Drama in Four Reels.

"A VOICE FROM THE SEA,"
A Kriterion Production

For Three Days, commencing THURSDAY JANUARY 18th:

"THE SECOND IN COMMAND."
A Rolfe-Metro, featuring Francis Bushman and Marguerite Snow

"IN SEARCH OF A HUSBAND,"
By Max Pemberton.

COMING SHORTLY,

The TANKS in the Battle of the Ancre.

See the Tanks in comfort AT

THE FINCHLEY RINK CINEMA

To the Accompaniment of good Music.

SEATS FOR ALL.   NO WAITING.

PRICES AS USUAL.

('Barnet Press' 13 November 1917)

CHAPTER 3

PROPAGANDA

From the early days the Government appreciated the need to control the output of information released to the British public. Initially rumours were rife – German soldiers bayoneting babies was one common myth - and nothing was done to dispel these. As early as September 1915 a meeting of leading writers was convened by the Government which included such luminaries as H G Wells, Thomas Hardy, James Barrie, Arthur Conan Doyle, Rudyard Kipling and John Buchan. Articles, cartoons and posters appeared which painted the Hun in an unflattering light, normally towering over a cowering mother or an unfortunate Belgian peasant.

(©IWMQ71309)

Of all the authors involved, John Buchan was the most active, producing a number of novels based on the war, *The Thirty Nine Steps* being the most famous. He was appointed Director of Information in 1917 reporting directly to the Prime Minister David Lloyd George and was responsible for a series of initiatives ranging from paintings by war artists to children's comics. One particular target audience was America whose early entry into the war would have been a great advantage; in the end this did not happen until 6 April 1917.

In 1915 the execution of Edith Cavell sparked outrage in Britain, and particularly the USA, and helped to raise support for the war. Edith was born in 1865 near Norwich and trained as a nurse at the London Hospital. She went to work in Belgium and when war broke out she was instrumental in sheltering over 200 British, French and Belgian soldiers and helping them to escape to Holland. She was arrested by the invading Germans, court martialled for treason, found guilty and, despite pleas from Britain, was executed by firing squad at 7.00am on 12 October 1915. Needless to say the British government made sure that Edith Cavell became an iconic figure and an example of German brutality.

('Barnet Press' 20 May 1916)

The monument to Edith Cavell in Charing Cross Road was erected in 1920. The inscription: "Patriotism is not enough. I must have no hatred or bitterness for anyone" were the words spoken by her on the eve of her execution.

The War Illustrated, 10th October, 1914. Registered at the G.P.O. as a newspaper.

Great Pen-Picture of the Battle of the Rivers by A. G. Hales See Page 183

The War Illustrated

2d Weekly

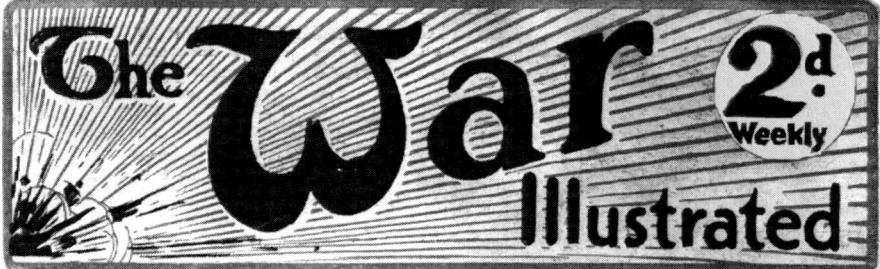

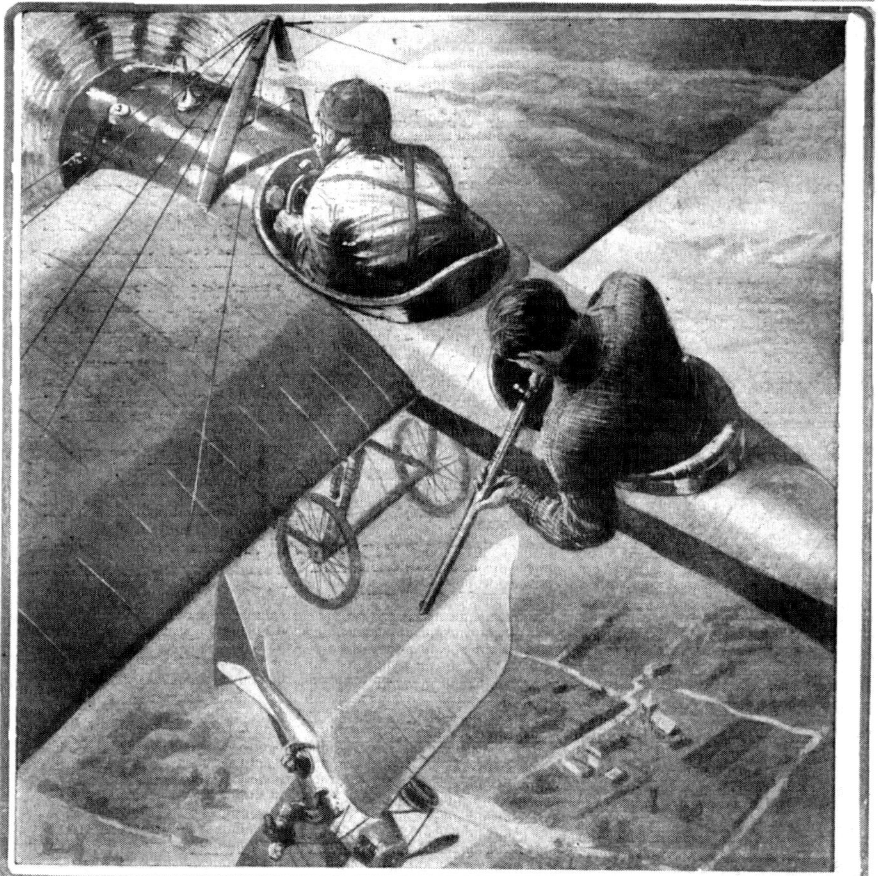

VOL. I., No. 8.

OUR TRIUMPHANT AIRMEN: A DUEL IN THE CLOUDS

Week ending 10 Oct. 1914

This was published by "Illustrated London News"

A particular innovation was the use of the new medium of cinema and a film was commissioned by the Government which was supposedly shot at the Front although it appears that some of the scenes might have been faked. *The Battle of the Somme* was released on 21 August 1916 and, at 75 minutes, was by far the longest film to be screened at the time. It played to huge audiences in theatres throughout the country and, despite the sometimes horrific scenes of dead and wounded soldiers in the trenches, it actually raised support for the war. Cinemas received priority in the supply of coal and electricity so they were places to go to when conditions at home were less than comfortable. Perhaps the most famous feature film was *Shoulder Arms* which appeared towards the end of the war in October 1918 and starred the ever popular Charlie Chaplin who also produced it.

Children were not to escape being targeted and a whole variety of comics, jigsaw puzzles, books and games were produced and aimed not only at boys but at girls too. Before the war Germany, and in particular Nuremberg, had been a leading producer of toys and games, and exports to Britain amounted to over £1 million. With a ban on imports, the home market was then supplied by British companies who made sure that their products were clearly labelled 'British Manufacture'

Children also played an important part in the war. The Boy Scout movement had been founded in 1908, and early in 1914 its founder Sir Robert Baden-Powell had said that he thought that that year they would be on the threshold of great developments. This proved to be a very accurate prediction for some 100,000 Scouts were pressed into service doing jobs that relieved the pressure on the military, including working on farms, running errands, carrying messages, collecting waste paper and tin cans. They also helped the police by cycling through the streets after an air raid and blowing the 'all clear' on their bugles.

They helped in rescue work and the Sea Scouts acted as coast watchers and signallers. The contribution of the Scouts was recognised by David Lloyd George who said in 1917:

Children's games

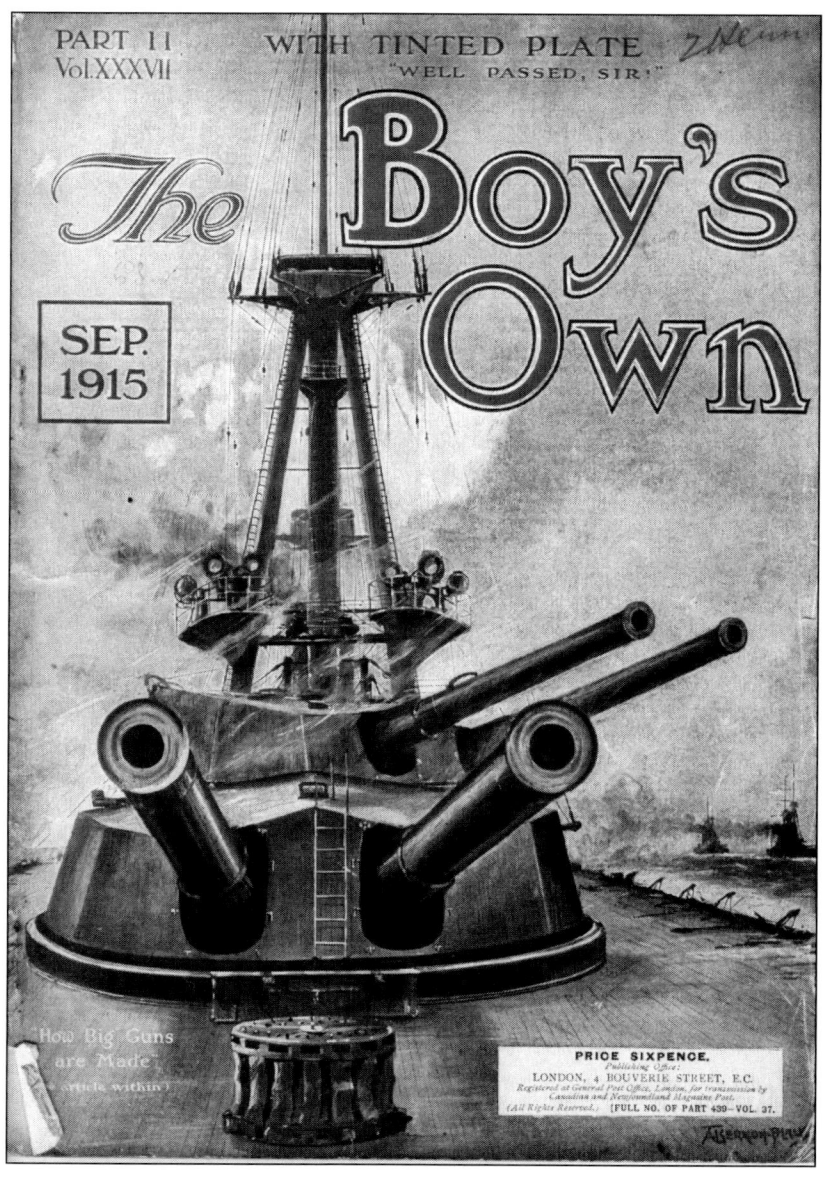

Even children's magazines had a war theme. In this particular issue there was an article on how to blow up a railway line, a tactic used by the Belgians to slow down the invading Germans

"I do not think I am exaggerating when I say that the young boyhood of our country, represented by the Boy Scouts Association, shares the laurels for having been prepared with the old and trusted British Army and Navy....within a month of the outbreak of war they were able to give the most energetic and intelligent help in all kinds of service. When the boyhood of a nation can give such practical proofs of its honour, straightness and loyalty, there is not much danger of that nation going under."

In 1918 responsibility for propaganda passed to a new department, the Ministry of Information, headed up by Lord Beaverbrook, but it was short lived as it was disbanded after the war.

Propaganda was not just confined to Government posters

Imperial Maritime League
2, Westminster Palace Gardens, Victoria Street, S.W.

KEEP THE FLAG FLYING

GERMAN ATROCITIES ON CHILDREN

The following atrocities are certified by the Belgian, French and British Governments, or by Dr. Arthur Jacques, Physician-in-Ordinary to H.M. the King of the Belgians, and are set forth in the Official Book of German Atrocities, the British Blue Book, or in the Supplement to "THE FIELD," of February 13th, 1915.

A Child Bayoneted.
On the 26th August, not far from Malines, a child of about fifteen was tied up, the hands behind the back, and the body was completely torn open with bayonet wounds (Official Book, p. 16).

Women and Children used as Screen.
On August 29th, at Herent, the Germans forced 500 women and children to march in front of their forces (Official Book, p. 69).

Women and Children Burnt.
In Tamines many persons, including women and children, were burnt or stifled in their homes (Official Book, p. 79).

Murdered.
In the Faubourg de Neffe an old woman and all her children were killed in their cellar (Official Book, p. 81).

Abuse of Girl of Eleven.
On the 3rd September, at Suippes, a little girl of eleven was subjected for three hours to the lubricity of a soldier: he had taken her to an empty house, where he stuffed a handkerchief into her mouth to stop her cries (Official Book, p. 119).

Mutilation.
The village of Sommeilles was the scene of a terrible drama. When the War broke out Mme. X., whose husband is with the Colours, took refuge in a cellar belonging to a couple called Adnot, together with these latter and their four children, aged respectively eleven, five, four, and one-and-a-half years. A few days afterwards the bodies of all these unfortunate people were discovered in a pool of blood. Adnot had been shot, Mme. X. had her right breast and arm cut off, the little girl of eleven had a foot severed, the little boy of five had his throat cut. The woman X. and the little girl appeared to have been raped (Official Book, p. 122).

Little Boy and Babies Shot.
In the Faubourg de Nancy in Nomeny a little boy of ten and two little girls of three were shot. The little boy had the crown of his head blown off, and one of the little girls had her elbow almost severed (Official Book, p. 129).

Girl of 12 Outraged.
At Magnieres a German armed with a rifle obliged a young girl ——, aged 12 years, to accompany him into a room. He violated her twice, in spite of her protests and the cries for mercy kept up without ceasing (Official Book, p. 147).

Living Child Photographed on Heap of Dead.
At Dinant they wedged a little child, alive, mind you, on the top of a heap of corpses. They then photographed the gruesome exhibit ("Field" Supplement, p. 5).

Mother Forced to Bury her Murdered Child.
Again, a mother saw a child killed before her eyes, and the soldiers compelled the unhappy woman to bury the child in their presence ("Field" Supplement, p. 5).

Girls Outraged before their Parents' Eyes.
Under the command of Von Bieberstein at Elleweyt nearly all the young girls were violated before their parents' eyes ("Field" Supplement, Feb. 13, 1915, p. 4).

Baby Disembowelled.
At Haecht a child of 3 with its stomach cut open by a bayonet was lying near the house (British Report, p. 15).

Baby Crucified.
And a child of 2 or 3 years old was found nailed to the door of a farmhouse by its hands and feet (British Report, p. 18).

From a Private attached to the Headquarters Staff.
"I believe if men at home could see the mothers running, with their dead children towards the fields, and if they could see the women and children lying smashed to pieces in their own homes, perhaps it might teach them to act the man!
"And it might appeal to others not to leave us in the lurch. We must have SHELLS! SHELLS!! SHELLS!!! for without them we can do nothing."

SAVE US FROM THE HUNS.

J. WOODROFF & SONS, WANDSWORTH.   No. 22.

CHAPTER 4

LETTERS FROM THE FRONT

Soon after the outbreak of war, the *Barnet Press* offered to send copies of the paper to troops serving abroad and it also encouraged people to send in letters received from their friends and relatives in the forces:

> WE invite those of our readers who have friends and relatives serving as soldiers with the British Expeditionary Force to send to the Barnet Press any letters they may receive from the front.
>
> The letters should be accompanied by the envelope in which they are received, together with the name, rank, and regiment of the writer, and the name and address in full of the person to whom they have been written. The letters will be returned in the same condition as received.

One such letter was received by a Mr A C Tilley of Oakleigh Park and was published in the issue of 9 January 1915:

> "I have just received your letter of the 9th inst., and was very interested in the news contained in it. We have not been in the trenches since I wrote last, but we have been under shell fire in this village, and in the wood near here. We (the artillery) had been shelling the Germans hard all day long, so they sent back a few 'souvenirs'. One shell burst in the front garden of a house opposite us, but did not do any damage. When the shells were being sent a little further down the street we went out and listened to them coming, and watched them burst. Don't think we were reckless, as it

was quite safe. The worst part, by far, of the affair was to see the scared villagers running about the street, wondering whether to take shelter. It is not a sight I want to see again. This morning when I was on a fatigue in the wood the Germans shelled a spot about 100 yards or less away from us, and the fragments of shell fell very close to us. I saw some 'Jack Johnsons' for the first time the other day, when the 'Allemands' put about 20 of them into a chateau (or rather what was a chateau) about 400 yards away from where I was. They were trying to find a battery of ours, but were not successful; as soon as they stopped shelling the battery opened fire on them. They are really terrible things, but I am glad I have been able to see some of them and know they are doing no damage. We are still billeted in the 'estaminet', and are not wanting to be moved yet……I will finish now, with the usual wish that you will all keep well, and that I may hear from you as often as possible. With much love…..If, by any chance, no letter comes from me during the near future, don't get anxious."

The reference to 'Jack Johnsons' would have been well understood at the time, although now it is lost in the mists of time. The German 150mm heavy artillery shells produce a cloud of black smoke when they exploded, thus reminding the troops of the famous black American world heavyweight champion boxer, Jack Johnson, 'The Galveston Giant'. Another reference to them had appeared in a letter of 3 December 1914:

"In answer to your letter requesting particulars of Sergt. C. Horton's death. I have gathered in every detail to the best of my ability, as I might tell you I had just left the trenches to join headquarters just previous to the sad occurrence. I will now explain how poor Charlie was killed. His Company were at the time in the front trenches, about 400 yards from the German trenches. We had been there for about 24 days, continually stopping the German attacks, chiefly at night. Well, it was on the day we were to be relieved for a little rest when the sad occurrence happened. Sergt. Horton, my comrade, was

> serving some men their rations for the day. He was, I might add, in the best of spirits, and was also quite undisturbed by the German shells falling practically everywhere. These shells we call 'Jack Johnsons.' Now, just as he was giving the last portion of rations to four men, a 'Jack Johnson' came and burst right into the trench, about two or three yards from where Charlie was. When the smoke had cleared away, alas! Poor Charlie's head was almost blown to pieces, and the other four men were either killed or wounded by the same shell. We, I might say, had lost 51 men the day previous in the same Company Charlie was in. Poor Charlie of course was killed (death being instantaneous) about 7.30 that eventful morning. Owing to strict censorship of letters, I regret I cannot tell you the name of the place he was killed, but I think you can obtain this information from the War Office. You have my deepest sympathy on your bereavement."

Apparently Sergeant Charles Thomas Horton, who was with the 1st. Battalion, Middlesex Regiment, was killed on 8 November 1914 and was buried at La Boutillerie.

In July 1915 Mrs Linsey of Porch Cottages, Oakleigh Road, Whetstone received the following letter from her son:

> "Just a line to let you know that I am on the RMS Ivernia, wounded to the head, after a terrible battle on the hills. We don't yet know if we will get off or not. We are at present at _____. We made a great charge and advance, under very heavy 'Jack Johnson' fire. We won the day but it cost us thousands of men. How it has finished I do not know. I only know that we had a struggle to climb over the dead Turks and Germans. We took many prisoners, and captured guns and ammunition. Fifteen thousand of our shells were fired before we started the advance, and when the Turks saw our bayonets they ran for their lives, throwing hand grenades behind them, and then by the time we reached the grenades they burst. During this bombardment all you could see were arms, legs ands machine guns

being blown up 50 feet into the air. There are 1500 of us on this ship now, and I know that there are thousands more waiting and also the_____, but none are coming to England. By the time you get this letter I hope to be back in the trenches again, as I am going on grand. The only trouble is I have the sound of the guns in my head. The worst sight was to see five of my mates blown to pieces around me. And me the only one missed. We have lost our officers and most of the sergeants, and the Manchester's, who were attached to us."

A letter in January 1915 from Rifleman W Ridden, 'B' Company, 1st Battalion Queen's Westminster Rifles to his parents in Bowes Park:

"It is very cold. The water in my bottle was a solid chunk yesterday. I had quite a decent Christmas on the whole. Stand to arms at 6.30a.m., when we sang "God Save the King," and "Deutschland über Alles" in compliment to our enemies. They replied with cheers, etc. We then lit nightlights and candles arranged all along the top of the trenches for decoration, and sang carols. The Germans and ourselves then did as we liked, walked about on the top and in front of the trenches, and not a shot was fired all day. We exchanged cigarettes and grub, shook hands, and some exchanged addresses to write to each other after the war. They sang some German carols, one of which I had heard just twelve months before played by a German band at Crouch End. We helped bury each other's dead in the afternoon, six men and one officer of each side going out to do it. Certainly I shall remember this Christmas Day as long as I am spared to live, as the most extraordinary one possible. We came out of the trenches at 4.30 on Boxing morning. I had heaps more grub to eat than it was possible to manage. For breakfast I had cold ham and tongue, the latter provided by my hutch companion, bread, jam, and hot café au lait. Dinner: Meat, potatoes, haricots, carrots and onions – all together in a tin, with the natural juice (fat and jelly). I soon heated it up and made a good stew. We had some more tongue,

Christmas pudding, dates, figs, muscatels, and almonds, chocolates, and many other sweets. To finish up I had a piece of the wounded cake (a gift from home which received a bullet when the writer left it momentarily on top of the trench) for tea and some hot café au lait. On the whole quite a satisfactory day. It didn't rain, but froze like a brick, and the air was very still and everything coated thick with hoar frost. By the way, the Germans challenged us to a game of football, which our officers, however, did not see fit to allow. They came from a town which I know is keen on footer. Keep cheerful and well. You can't stop shells and shot coming over, however anxious you get, so you must simply forget all about the risks. After all, I might have been scuppered by a motor-bus or bike accident before this, especially now all lights are prohibited in London."

Not every letter was as cheerful though. Lance-sergeant Geoffrey Tilley, No 1 Company, 13th Battalion County of London Regiment, British Expeditionary Force wrote to his parents in North Bank, Oakleigh Park in January 1915:

"I am still alive and going strong; keeping in good spirits too. We left the rest camp last Tuesday morning, marched to the station, and entrained for our present station. We were loaded like sheep in real cattle trucks, marked 'Chevaux 8; hommes 36-40." In our truck we had about 35, I suppose, chiefly sergeants. The journey was the most uncomfortable, and at the same time the most marvellous journey I have ever made. We were in the train about 24 hours and travelled at an average of about 15 miles per hour. That meant we had to sleep on the train, and there was just about room for everyone to lie down; the floor was completely covered. If one man moved, he disturbed about four or five others. It was very cold too. But on the whole I quite enjoyed the journey; everything was so novel. Our rations consisted of Bully-Beef, jam and biscuits. Arrived at our destination, we marched to our present billet – an empty chateau. Here we are quite comfortable. We have been here about three days now. The work is quite easy. Reveille at 7, and lights out at 9. Up to the present we have done chiefly route marching. The weather here is mild and rainy; it has rained off and on since we have been here. We can hear the guns from the Front in the evening, when it is quiet. There is a complete lack of English tobacco, cigarettes and matches in France, as the Government have the monopoly of all these things. French cigarettes, etc. are absolutely rotten. The one thing I seem to miss in France is good tobacco. I know you will send me some if you have not already done so. I should also like a tinder lighter, which you can obtain at any tobacconist. I have not tasted any Christmas pudding this year, and it would be a great treat if you could manage to send one. I am longing to get a letter from someone at home. Love to all."

Second Lieutenant T Kirkham Jones wrote to his parents on 18 January 1915 to give them a detailed description of conditions in a trench:

"…..I have been reading the letters on page 7 of the 'Barnet Press' and the majority of the writers are in the same portion of the firing line as ourselves, and all they say of the trenches is quite true. By the way, I have got a topping 'dug out' this time, 5ft. 8in. by 4ft. deep, in which Second Lieutenant Nightingale and I grub together, and in which I and my servant sleep. The roof consists of two-inch planking, with about three feet of earth on top. The last occupant left a plate-glass mirror behind 2½ft. by 1½ft., and since I came into the trench again my servant, hearing there was a spring mattress to be had in the ruined farmhouse 100 yards in front of our trench, collared it, and I am now sleeping on it. My table is a trench footboard 4ft. by 18in. by 18in. high, which was too clumsy to walk on, so I had it brought into my little house. Everything inside is arranged to a nicety and my Webb equipment is hung from two nails on the left-hand side of my head. My revolver I have in an entrenching tool carrier under the water bottle. My rifle is hung over my head as I sleep, and my gumboots stand at the foot of the bed, ready to be slipped on as I tumble out of bed. A ration box, supported by two pegs driven into the side of the dug-out, makes an excellent shelf in which to keep all the groceries. The floor is covered a foot deep in straw from a neighbouring stack, and any water, of which there is plenty, drains into a hole from which it is bailed. My fireplace is an old bucket, in which some holes have been punched with an entrenching tool, and the coke and charcoal, with which we are supplied, burn championly in it. We are quite well off for crockery, etc., all of which the servants found in the old farmhouse only about 50 yards from the Germans, and caught a rabbit and a chicken, which have now been eaten. The snipers have been particularly busy today, and I have been unfortunate enough to have a sergeant of my platoon hit, but only slightly wounded. I told you of the shelling our people gave the German trenches the other day. It was beautiful, and our fellows were fairly shouting with joy. The Germans always retaliate by shelling the town. Please do all you can to let me have the trench jacket, and especially the waterproof trousers. At the present minute I am soaking wet; as you are walking down the trenches in the dark, you scrape all the mud off the sides, and the bottom of the Burberry seems to have a habit of always getting into every drop of water you get near to. The list of things you are sending me is excellent, and it is really jolly good of you. If you could send a little sauce as well, it would be just the thing for the soup. It is better, I think, to send the things in small parcels than in one large one. Please do not put 'Base Depot' on any address in future, it causes delay, and we never go to the base."

Although the reference to his 'servant' may make it appear that he was an aristocrat, in fact the official army term for someone who was assigned to help an officer was 'soldier-servant', more commonly known as a 'batman'.

The true horrors of the war were recorded in this letter in the same issue of *Barnet Press*. W. Elliot of Queen Victoria Rifle (9th County of London) wrote to his brother at 27 Park View Crescent, New Southgate:

"We are having it rather thick. I have just come out of the trenches after being there three days and nights, and, my word, the terrors of these places are unspeakable, especially at this time of the year. This appears to be their wet season; it is raining practically every day, and the head cover of the trenches gets considerably battered

An-on Loose Fitting Underwear

Vermin Proof

Men in the trenches write stating that "An-on" Silk Underwear is proof against vermin.

British Made.

Sold by High Class Outfitters all the world over.

Built on anatomical lines. Is loose to the body, and allows a freedom impossible in close-fitting garments.

BUTTONS LIKE A COAT.

There is a special fulness in the DRAWERS and UNION SUITS that is highly appreciated by men of active habits.

Perfect in quality, wear and workmanship. Made in Drawers, Vests, and UNION SUITS for Men, Boys, and Girls.

	Vests.	Drawers.	Suits.
Silk, *from*	7/6	7/6	12/6
Taffeta ,,	7/6	7/6	12/6
Cotton ,,	3/6	3/6	5/6

The An-on Union Suit

An-on Underwear.

Comfort in the trenches

by the constant downpour. So, that being the case, we have to stick in a stooping position, which makes one very cramped. One of our officers happened to stand upright, and got a bullet right in his head. So you imagine the terrible strain upon the constitution of the fellows. They gave us a nice bit of rifle fire on New Year's Eve, exactly at midnight. We could hear them singing and playing bugles. But as soon as it was light on January 1st we got it hot with shell fire. One Company of our Battalion was behind in a barn, in reserve, when two shells struck it, killing 11 men and wounding 30 or more, that being the heaviest loss of ours since here. This country is more devastated than France. One place we passed through to the trenches has only part of the church left."

The following day he wrote again to his brother with more bad news:

"Just a few lines to let you have some sad news. To-day we have lost poor Bowden, one of Cook, Son, and Company boys. We were at a village resting for three days previous to going into the trenches again, when the Germans sent over two shells almost in succession. On hearing the first explosion, some of our chaps rushed out to see what was happening, when another burst in front of him and blew him into small pieces. Poor fellow! About other casualties, you must get these from the papers. I put up a cross just as a last tribute to him. I cannot write more now, as I feel too upset. It all happened about 30 yards down the street away from our billet, where we are staying."

A letter dated 15 February 1915 contained an intriguing reference to the modern aspects of warfare:

"We have been greatly amused by the air fights which are continually going on round here. The air is swarmed with English, French, Belgian and German planes and as soon as a German 'plane appears, the guns open fire and drop shells all round it. We have not

> seen one hit yet, though we are expecting to. These 'planes fly very high up, almost out of fire."

The British planes would have been from the Royal Flying Corps (RFC), a branch of the British Army. The RFC first used aeroplanes on 13 September 1914, and then purely for aerial spotting, so this reference must have been one of their first instances of their being used in aerial combat. German planes were also active as this letter written from the Front on 6 December 1915 shows:

> "This morning, just after eight, two German aeroplanes came over here, dropping bombs. They are using, evidently, a new kind of bomb for they are far more destructive than the ones that have before been dropped here. Eleven of our men – North Lancashire's – were killed. They have only been here a few days, too, and are waiting to advance. A father, mother and their two little girls were killed, also another mother and little girl. I went into the mortuary to see the bodies, and they were in a frightful state – riddled and torn with pieces of shell. It was too terrible to describe. A chum who was with me, a married man, had tears in his eyes when he saw the poor little girl lying dead, and said to me, 'I can't help it, Nick, I've got kiddies of my own'. I afterwards went to look at the house where the people were living when the bomb struck it. The roof was half off and all the windows out, and inside there was not a wall which was not cracked, or a door which was not touched by the bullets from the shell. An old man of 80, perhaps more, was walking about half demented, vowing all sorts of vengeance on 'les Boches.' It was his daughter and his child who were lying on a bed in a pool of blood dead. Can the people of England believe that such things are happening? Can they wonder that the French will not hear of peace on terms? Anyhow, the Huns soon paid the price for the terrible cold-blooded murder they had done, for both the aeroplanes were brought down soon after."

The letter concluded with an impassioned plea to civilians at home:

"How long is it before they are all going to be wiped out? How many more innocent women and children are going to be sacrificed to their lust for killing? Every available man is needed to wring the eagle's neck, and there are some thousands in England who should come now, before it is too late. Remember, boys, you will not only be fighting on the side of justice; you will be fighting for yourselves, for the existence of yourselves, your wives, and children. Your own home is at stake, don't some of you realise what is happening? Can't 'footer' stand by for a month or two? I play football myself every season, but I did not stop to think about it this year. I don't fight and I don't get chances to win V.C.'s, but I am doing my bit with a good heart, and I share the opinion of lots of others out here. i.e., there should be more work and less play in England just now. Now then lads, roll up all of you, and when the days work is done you will find that you have not lost anything, but rather gained a bit."

This latter part does not, however, seem to be the kind of thing that would be written by an average soldier to his family – could it have been planted by the authorities to encourage recruitment?

Whilst aeroplanes were the modern side of warfare, on the ground horses were still being used in vast numbers. This letter was received in June 1915: from the AVC Convalescent Home, Horse Depot, British Expeditionary Force:

"……..our work is very pleasant, for the cause is good, and the harmony that exists between the officers and men is marvellous. We have handled 27,000 horses in this depot since the war broke out and have had very few deaths. Those that have had to be destroyed have suffered nothing in the death, for the cattle killer is very sure and the look in their eyes gives you the idea that death is a relief to the poor brutes. This is only a receiving depot. We get some good long runs up the lines towards the frontier with the fit animals. Every animal is passed thoroughly before he leaves for the Front and great pains are taken to see that they do not get injured on the journey up. There are a few farms under this depot, which are commandeered by the Government for the grazing of the animals, which, after being dressed, are turned out to recuperate and get a rest. The winter was very rough, but there were very few horses lost considering the very hard winter it was and the majority being used to be kept inside and good beds, standing out, they weathered it very well indeed. They are now put in stables at night, the horses that are ready to go up to the Front, and are pegged out in lines in the daytime and brought in at night. There is only a cover for their heads. They are very well groomed and cleaned before they leave, and are all fit for the work they will be called upon to perform after they get to the fighting line. I must mention the R.S.P.C.A. have been a great boon to the A.V.C., being the donors of some very useful gifts such as removal vans for removing horses to hospital when they are so bad that it is necessary for us to cart them. They have also been the donors of horse-rugs, which were very useful last winter for the horses that needed them."

A letter to Mrs Percy Clarke of Rookwood, North Finchley from her son in February 1915 gives a good idea of the work performed behind the lines by the medical teams:

"I am writing this from the receiving room at the hospital our section have taken over for a fortnight. My business is simply to see that the patients reach here from the convoys, and then are taken to the wards to which they are detailed. Surgical cases are treated here first. Convoys arrived pretty frequently, and, as many of the wounded are on stretchers, the work is not light. Carrying on one's back people with bad feet is rather tiring too. It is very interesting to watch the treatment of the wounds, although the sight of them is often ghastly. We are on duty for 6 hours twice during the 24. My turns are from 9 till 3. I have lately been in charge of surgical ward No. 2, where cases are sent that are not serious – that is, not likely to die. The work there was always in rushes; the wounded came in all of a heap after being dressed. The two of us on duty had to put the man to bed, getting their wet boots and putties, and small tunics and shirts off, and giving them soup. You cannot imagine the amount of mud they have in their boots and socks, and on their overcoats and breeches. One often has to cut the clothes off with a knife. This fortnight is considered as a rest, although the work is really much more tiring. The rest is for one's nerves, I think. The last time we were out we went into a farmyard up to our knees in manure and mud. This all got inside my boots, and, although I have washed my feet every day, they burn like blazes. I expect you will get this in about 10 days, as the censor is the chaplain, and is, I am told busy with other work. We hear much talk about the conditions in the trenches. It must make life unbearable. It is bad enough for us."

Send your man a pen (advertisement in 'Bystander' 1917)

The reference to the chaplain is an interesting one. Despite the graphic and often harrowing descriptions in the letters from the Front at this time, there does not seem to have been any attempt to delete these. The censor's main job at this time was to ensure that no mention was made of actual place names, which could have aided the enemy. A green envelope was issued to troops who preferred that their immediate commander should not read their letters to censor them. A proportion of such letters – which the soldiers guaranteed to contain nothing censorable – was examined at the Base.

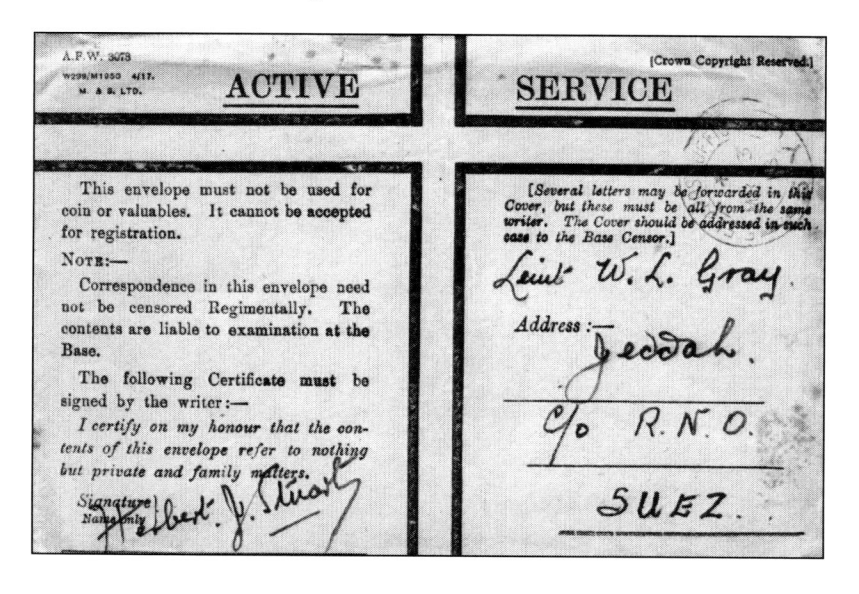

The army also issued Field-Service postcards on which a brief message could be written in haste. Letters to and from home, however harrowing, were considered to be good for the morale of the soldiers and it was only later in the war as the civilian population started to become more aware of the appalling conditions in the trenches and the needless slaughter, that letters ceased to be published in the press. In 1917 when several military setbacks were becoming worrying for the Government, all books and publications were subjected to censorship and 4000 censors were employed to monitor not only the press but mail as well.

The humour of the troops is nicely illustrated in this extract from a letter from a son to his parents in Beulah Lodge, Oakleigh Road:

"....we have fires for cooking. A fire is cheerful at all times, especially so in the trenches when rain falls in the daytime and the water freezes at night. During our time of rest we have a sleep in our dugout; that is if we can get warm. When we hear the British shells bursting in the German trenches, we look out from our own trenches. Our men seem cheerful in the trenches. When a German sniper gets to work someone shouts out, 'Now then, Fritz, if you don't put that toy down I shall have to come and take it away from you.' Our boys give them a few parodies – not very complimentary...!"

A Field Service postcard

Perhaps one of the most frightening weapons in the war was poison gas which was first used by Germany on 22 April 1915. Allied soldiers were initially puzzled at a thick yellowish green mist coming towards them from the German lines. The effects were appalling – gagging and choking, convulsions and, in severe cases, death. The gas was chlorine and this would later be supplemented by mustard gas which was contained in shells and caused massive internal and external blisters in both humans and horses.

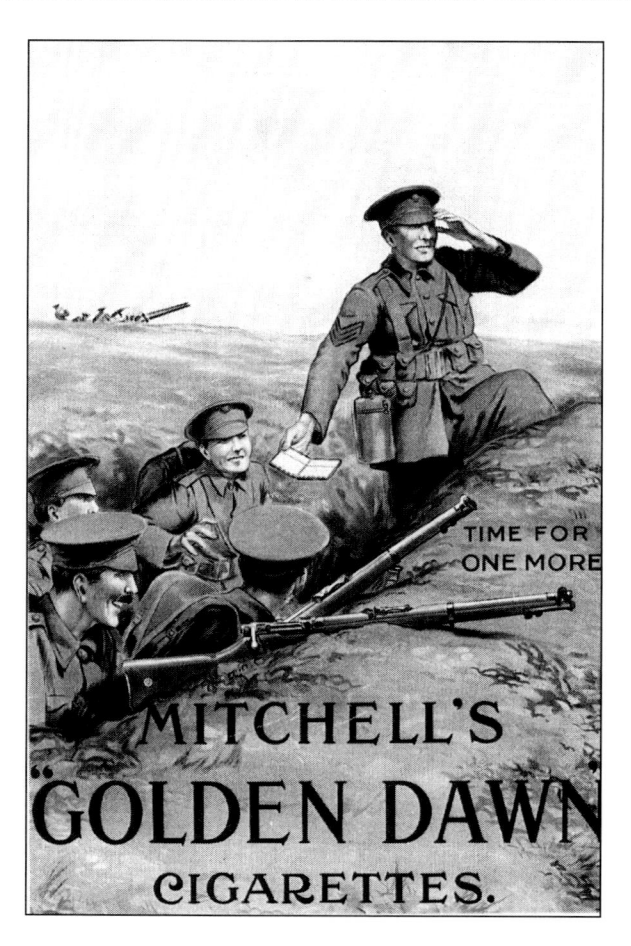

An almost unbelievable advertisement from 1915. Handing out cigarettes while standing up in a trench was not recommended

DAILY NEWS LETTER.

7th JULY, 1916.

British News.—Admiral Jellicoe's despatch has now been published. In it he places the German losses at two battleships of the Dreadnought type, one of the Deutschland type, five light cruisers, six destroyers and a submarine. All these were seen to sink. Further, two battle cruisers, one battleship of the Dreadnought type and three destroyers were seen to be so severely damaged that their return to port is extremely doubtful. One of these latter, the *Lutzow* is admittedly sunk.

The fifth day of the Franco-British offensive continues to develop favourably for the Allies. Total number of German prisoners taken by the Allies since the commencement of the battle is 15,500.

The Germans grudgingly admit that the French and British have met with certain successes on the Somme.

The Kaiser has passed through Cologne on his way to the Western front. The inference is obvious.

Mr. Asquith stated in the House of Commons that it was in no way desirable to give any information at present as to the strength, movements or intentions of the British.

8 A.M., JULY 7TH.—General Haig reports that the British have made a further slight advance near Thiepval. South of La Bassée Canal, after a discharge of smoke gas, we made several successful raids on the German lines. Among the regiments which specially distinguished themselves were the Royal Welsh Fusiliers and the Highland Light Infantry, who raided the German trenches, destroyed several mine shafts and inflicted 200 casualties on the enemy.

Low clouds interfered with aviation, but a British machine in the Tsapuvme area, dropping to 300 feet, successfully bombed a train from which German reinforcements were alighting. A British battery in another area secured several direct hits on a German battery and a battalion in column of route, inflicting many casualties.

Russian News.—To-day's Petrograd communiqué says that the Russians have had many local successes from Riga to the Carpathians, notably near Baranovichi where a thousand prisoners were taken, and again on the right bank of the Dneister.

The German forces under von Bothmer have retired from their old positions in the Barysz sector to the river Koropiec, ten miles West of the Strypa. The Petrograd General Staff estimate the Austrian losses during the past month alone at more than half a million men.

Russian guns at a range of four miles are pounding away at Baranovichi on three sides, and Hindenburg is frantically trying to prevent the envelopment of his right wing opposite Lutzk.

[P.T.O.

Some British troops were kept abreast of the war news.
This News Letter was issued in Cairo

BARKER "KENBAR" TRENCH COAT

John Barker and Company, Ltd

(Reg. No. 328601)

The Coat the Officer will have.

WITH collar which can be worn in three positions. The "Kenbar" is a great favourite amongst Officers, and can be thoroughly relied upon. Absolutely proof against any weather, and guaranteed waterproof. Made from our noted trebly-proofed KENBAR-CORD. Lined throughout proofed check woollen and interlined waterproof, not oiled silk. Every detail so necessary for the strenuous wear in the trenches is embodied in this Coat. It has reinforced elbows, which are absolutely essential, and full skirt with cavalry gusset. The "Kenbar" is the finest cut and best tailored Trench Coat in London.

Every Officer should wear a "Kenbar."

Cut with Raglan sleeves and very easy armholes, and can easily be slipped on over a British Warm. Send your order at once mentioning only chest measurement taken over Service Jacket, and a perfect fit is guaranteed.

94/6

With detachable Fleece lining, **126/-**. Supplied (as sketch) with detachable Fur Collar of Wallaby, **20/-** extra. Good quality Fleece Undercoats for wearing under Trench Coats at **35/-**. These are greatly in demand, and very warm and cosy.

We supply Fur Collars as sketch separately. Officers can very easily attach them to their Trench Coats. Prices as follow :—
Good quality Wallaby - - - **20/-** each.
Best quality Natural Musquash - **35/-** ,,
,, ,, Nutria - - - **35/-** ,,
These collars are greatly in demand, and indispensable for Trench wear.

JOHN BARKER & CO. Ltd., Kensington, W.8

The standard issue British Army greatcoat was not waterproof and consequently absorbed both mud and water. Superior versions were available for those who could afford them.
(Advertisement in 'Bystander' December 1917)

A letter in the *Barnet Press* of 5 June 1915 described one victim:

> "Just a few lines to say I am getting on fine after my illness. I was gassed on Hill 60, on May 8th, and we had a rough time of it. The Germans sent the gas over to us, and we had to leave the trenches. After that the wind changed round and gave them some. But they lost more, and when the reinforcements came up they said they were fed up. So we made a charge and gave them something. We took 20 of them, and they told us they did not want to fight, and asked us for water. I am sorry to say the Bedfords are having a rough time of it out there. I am in Liverpool Hospital. I am getting on fine, and hope to be home soon and also soon to have a shot at the Germans again. It was just like shooting birds, so many of them."

Fortunately the Forces' Post Office was well organised and dealt with huge volumes of mail so the British Tommy could write regularly to his wife, mother or sweetheart. At this time postcards were in their heyday and there were numerous varieties ranging from those with regimental badges to the more sentimental with such messages as "I Miss You More Than Words Can Tell" or "Greetings From France."

*Embroidered silk postcards were hugely popular,
This one features the flags of the Allies*

A conventional postcard from 1918

CHAPTER 5

LETTERS FROM HOME

A resident of Friern Barnet, Anthea Gray, has a collection of over 200 letters written during the war by her mother, Mabel Broughton Holman, who lived at 16 Wilton Road, Muswell Hill along with her mother, Caroline Holman, sisters Winifred and Hilda and brother, Gerald.

Mabel wrote to William Lionel Gray every week between 1914 and 1918 with letters of anything up to ten pages. Lionel was in the Westminster Dragoons on manoeuvre on Salisbury Plain at the outbreak of war, and was posted immediately to Egypt. The Westminster Dragoons were the first unit in the British Army to be equipped with wireless apparatus – carried on pack horses.

Mabel was 28 when war broke out and she and William had met and fallen in love when they were working for Bentley's, a coding firm in the City of London. In the early years of the 20th century telegraph messages were charged by the number of words used, so a method of encoding phrases into one word was invented, thus saving money. For example a phrase "we have sold 500 tons July/August Antwerp £1 2s 6d" would be encoded RUCONEJA, where RU means "we have sold", CO means 500 tons, N means July/August, E means Antwerp and JA means £1 2s 6d, from a list of prices.

Lionel took part in the defence of the Suez Canal against the Turks and after a period of patrolling Cairo against the rioters there he was posted to Gallipoli and took part in the action against the Turks across the Salt Lake, being then in charge of a machine gun section. His regiment was then recalled to Egypt and re-equipped as Cavalry to deal with the revolt of the Senussi. Gray's experience in coding was put to good use in the Army when he became assistant to T. E Lawrence and prepared maps and ciphers of Palestine preparatory to General Allenby's "big push". Later he was sent to G.H.Q. Ismailia and thence on a secret mission with Lawrence to Jeddah. He was in Jeddah in 1918 when war ended.

Mabel's letters to Lionel, whom she nicknamed "Golliwog" on account of his curly hair, mainly contain items of personal interest, but she also describes events occurring at home. Some extracts help to give a feeling of how things were in London at the time. When William left home to join up the couple were not yet engaged, but in a letter of 20 August 1914 she describes her feelings after he had given her an engagement ring:

"My darling sweetheart

I must just write and tell my Golliwog what a proud little girl I am today and how delighted I am with the beautiful ring. I can hardly realise what it all means yet - it seems so strange – but it's a very nice feeling to be real sweethearts and I hope, dear, you will always have occasion to be proud of me – I will do my best and try to be worthy of your trust in me. I did not really see it myself till we got in the train and then I was quite dazzled. It was some time before Gerald saw it and mother did not at all till we told her. I could not sleep last night, as I was much too excited. It was a pity I had to go so quickly from you and I hope we shall get a few hours together tonight or tomorrow to our little selves – I am writing this in case we do not, but I do hope we can. The few sweet moments were too short, but I shall never forget them or under the trees in the Mall – what a night that was, the strangest you or I will ever spend, with all the sounds of war in the air and the horrible feeling of dread of what was going to happen, mixed with the sweetest feelings that any human being has ever experienced.

I must stop this or you will be saying "what an imaginative sweetheart I have."

You did not say if you wished me to wear it in the office, but I have it on and hide it when I go in to E L B. So far no one has spotted it. I will wait here for a phone message from you tonight.

I must not stop to write more now.

With much love and kisses

Yours ever

Cherry Bobs

My first letter in my new character!"

The two sweethearts, Mabel and Lionel

Not surprisingly, a newly engaged young girl who was separated from her beloved would feel frustrated and unhappy and this is a recurring theme in her letters. On 2 September 1914 she wrote to him at the Westminster Dragoons training camp in Pirbright:

> "I am most disappointed at not coming down to see you – as it is now we shall not get 5 minutes to ourselves. I did think you would like to have me, I really don't see it will serve any purpose my going to your home tomorrow night – just to sleep – I had heaps to talk to you about and you don't reciprocate at all. If you are always going to put others first it will not lead to any happiness I can assure you. I feel very hurt about it….."

Three weeks later she wrote:

> "…I had a miserable dream – I came to meet you and you were so cool – just shook hands and passed away. I woke up with a shock. It was thinking so much yesterday about wishing we had been married before you left. One thing made me very worried and that was – well I hardly like to put it in a letter. Anyway I'm not getting younger. Perhaps you can put two and two together and follow my thoughts."

On 12 October 1914 her misery was again highlighted;

> "Sunday I had the reaction and spent most of the day in the bedroom in tears. I'm up one day and down the next. It's the first time since you went though that I have broken down altogether and I have been strung up for weeks and weeks. I feel very done up today in consequence. The news too is bad – Antwerp having fallen. It seems terrible - I really cannot bear to read about it…. I'm beginning to think it's the end of the world and that we shall all be killed; for surely if there is any religion now is the time to prove it and punish those who are to blame for such wickedness. If I am to die, I should like to be with you, so we will see how things go and if they do not get better, we must arrange something, as I'm sure you share my feelings in the matter."

On his departure to the Middle East she sent him the following telegram:

As well as the weekly letters to each other they also exchanged parcels of gifts and it says much for the efficiency of the Forces Postal Service that these nearly always arrived intact, although there were often periods where several letters would be delivered together, possibly because they were held up at base camp. On his first Christmas away Mabel sent William a Christmas pudding and a khaki shirt. She would send Christmas puddings every year and in return he would send her many postcards of Egypt as well as ethnic gifts which Mabel put in her bottom drawer, with the intention of creating an Egyptian room in their future home. They also exchanged photographs, with him sending her the films themselves which she would have developed at Kodak in London. She was among many such visitors to their shop and in 1915 Kodak offered to develop and print selected photographs from soldiers free of charge.

In Mabel's early letters she reported the influx of Belgian refugees into London:

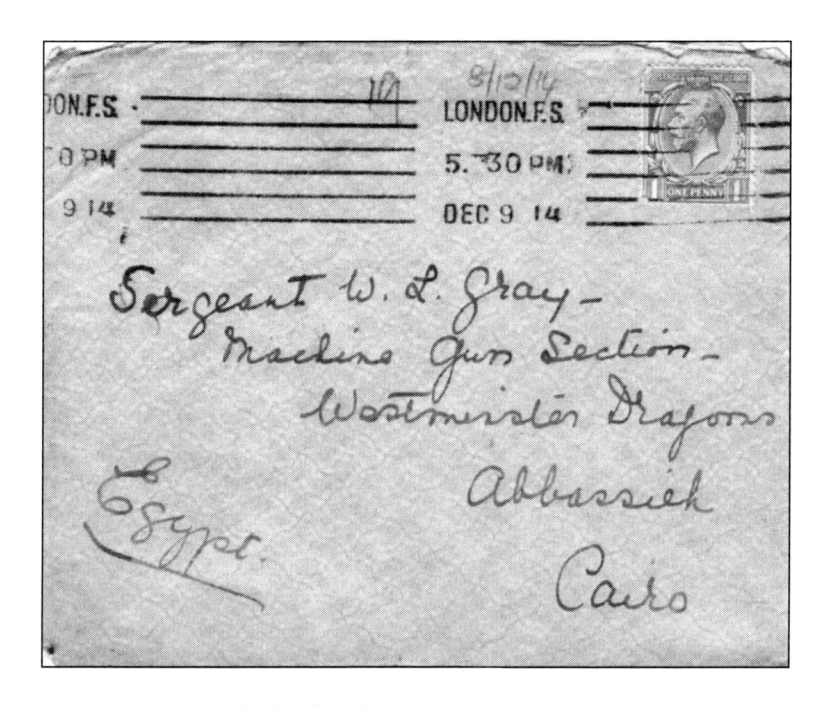

Mabel's first letter to Lionel in Egypt

Mail was forwarded to wherever he was stationed

MAILS LOST AT SEA.

The Postmaster-General announces that the following Mails have been lost at sea through enemy action:—

(1) A Parcel Mail for the Salonica Force containing parcels for that Force which reached the Army Post Office, London, for despatch between 6 p.m. on June 12 and noon on June 17.

(2) Mails for the Egyptian Expeditionary Force containing letters, packets, and newspapers (but not parcels), which reached the Army Post Office, London, for despatch between 3 30 p.m. on May 31 and 2 30 a.m. on June 4, and letters only which were received for despatch between 3 30 p.m. on June 7 and 2 30 a.m. on June 9.

(3) Mails for Egypt, Seychelles, Mauritius, Madagascar and Reunion containing correspondence which reached the General Post Office, London, for despatch as follows:—

Destinations and dates on which the lost correspondence was received at the General Post office.

EGYPT AND SEYCHELLES.

Letters.	Printed Matter.
June 1 and 2 and June 8	May 31 to June 2 and on June 7 and 8

MAURITIUS.

May 30 to June 8	May 30 to June 8

MADAGASCAR, REUNION, &c.

May 20 to June 8	May 20 to June 8

(4) Letter and Parcel Mails from Australia, Ceylon, Aden and Egypt, which left Adelaide on May 22, Fremantle on May 27, Colombo on June 13, Aden on June 22, and Port Said on June 30.

Not all letters reached Egypt intact

CHEAP TELEGRAMS TO FRONT.

Arrangements have been made for weekend letter-telegrams of a social character to be sent to or from soldiers, sailors, and nurses in this country, France, and Belgium, the various extra European British possessions, Egypt and the Persian Gulf. The charges will be approximately one-fourth of those for ordinary telegrams.

Telegrams of inquiry concerning casualties or the progress of persons officially reported seriously wounded or ill in over-sea possessions will be transmitted by the telegraph companies free of charge.

Cables would get through, but even at reduced rates, were expensive

"Going home on Tuesday a gentleman got in my carriage who was returning from Brussels!! He said the soldiers were splendid – the wounded and worn out ones were returning from the last fight on Saturday and some were walking along asleep – they were so done up. The spies were being shot by hundreds. One woman was walking along with a baby and round the baby was a plan of Liege. Another had a wireless set on her breast. The statues in the town had been also set up with wireless. He said we should have to do the same with our spies – shoot them and he was going to write an article in the paper when he had time on his experiences." *(13 August 1914)*

16 Wilton Road, which would be almost unrecognisable to Mabel (Author)

"We have about 1200 Belgian refugees at the Alexandra Palace – poor people, old, infirm and their homes gone. The public are not admitted, but you can send them clothes, etc." *(16 September 1914)*

"At Finsbury Park there was a SE & E train full of Belgian refugees, poor people, with no hats and only a few bundles of clothes with them. They were going to the Alexandra Palace." *(7 October 1914)*

"We have seen some of the Belgian refugees from the Palace and spoke to some the other morning. They wanted to go to the Bank and asked us the way. Poor wretched people – no homes, no money." *(19 October 1914)*

"I think we are going to have German prisoners at the Alexandra Palace, now the Belgian refugees have left." *(19 April 1915)*

"The Palace is now full of German prisoners and I hope they don't get out. Everyone feels rather nervous now." *(16 May 1915)*

She also mentioned the increasing presence of troops in the streets of London:

"It seems quite true about the Russian soldiers – we have had it confirmed from ever so many sources – a firm here in London had a telephone call today from Avonmouth to say the place was full of them – Archangel is where they come from. Another man could not make out why it was so much coal was going to Archangel! 60,000 are already at Ostend and about 40,000 more are en route! Isn't it great! I could jump for joy! Don't tell anyone though as it is a great secret yet. Won't the Germans have a surprise, I should think it would cause a panic when they see them because they won't know where they come from or how many there are behind them. I think it's a clever move." *(26 August 1914)*

"The atrocities are terrible, especially to the wounded. I heard of two separate cases – they are here in England. One had both legs shot off and while lying wounded his eyes were dug out with a bayonet. Another had both his hands cut off and his eyes dug out. His brother went to see him and was not allowed to. Isn't it too horrible to even think of them – surely they will not be allowed to continue this and will be punished for it if there is any justice in this world." *(28 September 1914)*

"I went to the pictures with mother in the evening to try and get cheered up, but you see so many now of the war – wounded soldiers and poor refugees that you come away feeling more depressed than ever." *(19 October 1914)*

"I saw, as I was leaving the office on Saturday, about 6 motor cars full of wounded – the first I have seen - it made me feel very bad. Some were leaning out, interested in their drive. One, a Scotchman, had evidently lost a hand and no-one gave them a cheer, simply stood and gaped at them. One old gentleman did wave and the Tommy looked so pleased. It takes something to rouse we English folk!! Of course, I think we feel it deep down inside us somewhere, at least I know I do, but we don't show it." *(23 November 1914)*

"I saw a soldier's funeral today in Lime Street. A motor hearse and coffin covered with a Union Jack. It was the Scots Greys. It was the first I had seen and made me feel so miserable. Poor feller." *(12 January 1915)*

"I went to a Sunday concert and heard some fine talent. Of course, all entertainments now have the patriotic element in them and the audience is nearly all soldiers getting leave and going out to enjoy themselves with their friends." *(11 February 1915)*

"Strange to say, ever so many soldiers were seen this weekend round our way with sun helmets on and evidently from abroad. They proved to be the 7th Middlesex back from Malta. They are now at Barnet and had lost their caps on the voyage home. Consequently were strolling about in pith helmets and drill suits." (*23 February 1915*)

"On Saturday afternoon I walked right up west and watched the drilling in Somerset House and then went to Buckingham Palace and Wellington Barracks - some of the National Guard were drilling there." *(3 March 1915)*

"Ernie went to a concert in Sandgate one night with a friend - returned home late to find themselves shut out, so he went down to the beach for a bathe, at 12 o'clock at night! He had only a handkerchief to dry himself on and managed to lose his identity disc on the beach. So he struck some matches to try and find it. Down came some soldiers and wanted to know what they were doing with lights on the beach. They had rather a job to clear themselves then they met a coastguard who came after the same thing and by all accounts he nearly got "turned in" *(3 March 1915)*

"I heard a gentleman last night talking about his son who had been 13 days in the trenches without respite – one had died there from exposure and two others had gone raving mad. I believe heaps are brought back in strait jackets – we heard this from a Naval Lieutenant who is on a hospital ship to and from France. Then the German and English dead were left in front of the trenches since last December! Whatever will it be like when the sun gets hot?" *(16 April 1915)*

"Conditions in the army are very different – not so much swank with the officers, most of whom have to make do on their pay and the moustache is no longer fashionable – too many youngsters in now for it to be possible, so rules are relaxed (good job too). *(16 June 1915)*

"I saw Kitchener when he came down to the Guildhall and quite by chance. Bentley asked me to go to the CSSA and order a carpet sweeper for the office. Just as I got to the Mansion House I was stopped by thousands of troops and three bands. I watched them pass (they were HAC and others who had been to the front) then I made my way up Queen Victoria Street and there were crowds waiting so I thought I might as well. I saw Carson and Churchill and then his Lordship. He looked splendid – just like a coloured picture postcard. I waved my kerchief and he saluted all around. They simply rushed for his car and he got a tremendous reception, but looked a trifle as if he did not want it. There were also a lot of motor buses with cheering wounded Tommies on top." *(12 July 1915)*

"Yesterday at lunch our Slater's girls told us that on Saturday next they were giving a "Tea, Concert & Fun" to 150 wounded from St Thomas's. She showed us the programme and menu most excellently got up. They phoned the National Volunteers and they are lending a lot of motors to bring them. Since Xmas the girls have saved £48 for this and are also giving them all a very nice present. Awfully decent of them. She asked Win and me if we would like to stay and see them and join in. We said we would but I am afraid in spite of the jolly concert it will be harrowing, She told us they gave one some time ago and there were such dreadful cases that they had to retire and have a howl, they couldn't start serving them. Win happened to see a few arrive that time and said how miserable they all looked and how dreadful some of the cases were. This time they are going to have everything as lively as possible when they arrive – band etc. We offered to give anything they required, but she thanked us ever so much and said they had more than enough of everything and enough money in hand for another time. These girls do seem sports; a lot have volunteered for all sorts of work." *(21 February 1917)*

"We went to see a lot of wounded soldiers. We stayed and thoroughly enjoyed ourselves – it was very sad to see them limping in, a lot with legs off, but the band struck up lively music and they were all in such good spirits that we could not feel depressed for long – we only had about an hour's entertainment. We had been plonked down at a table with about 60 of them and had tea. We soon got over our shyness and joked with them all and fed them. Win had a poor boy next to her who had been in it from the first and had never been home (Lancashire), lost his leg and had only been up three days after six months in hospital. He said that this was his first treat in years." *(28 February 1917)*

Mabel gave some illuminating insights into conditions in London, including problems with transport:

"We went to see "old Grumpy" – a very amusing play. The theatre was pretty full. The lights of London were nearly all out, however, and while we were waiting to go in we watched the searchlights on the Admiralty Arch. We passed a bus with a W.D on top – I suppose he is one left behind." *(21 September 1914)*

"I was in town till 7 last night. The streets were deserted all in darkness – Old Broad street particularly murky, with one solitary 4 wheeler going along – it looked like London 50 years ago." *(7 October 1914)*

"London is more gloomy than ever – more lights out and even the buses darkened. I could hardly see my way down Colney Hatch Lane. All the head-lights on motors too have to be out and it is really dangerous going about much late at night. Two of the waiting rooms on Stroud Green station have soldiers sleeping in them – I don't know what the idea is unless it is to guard the bridge. I'm beginning to think it's the end of the world and that we shall all be killed; for surely if there if there is any religion now is the time to prove it and punish those who are to blame for such wickedness. If I am to die, I should like to be with you, so we will see how things go and if they do not get better, we must arrange something, as I'm sure you share my feelings in the matter." *(12 October 1914)*

"An example of crass stupidity. The woman put our beautiful, much treasured and well respected electric kettle on the fire to boil and we arrived in the morning to find a sad and burnt out, blackened kettle reclining on the shelf, smelling horribly as its internal works had been burnt. Bang goes 2 guineas. If it was not so sad, I could laugh (privately, I am doing so now). A new one was purchased by the Estate, not so good as ours and the first thing it did was to spit fire and give me an electric shock. I gave a yell, it's only 200 volts, so now I approach it very warily. It has also distinguished itself by leaking before it was used." *(30 October 1914)*

"Our Broad Street line was shut up suddenly yesterday and will be all day today which means, I suppose, more troops moving." *(14 November 1914)*

"We had a terrific storm last night – wind and snow – I have never heard anything like it. Win came home with her umbrella torn to shreds and it beat the snow in all our rooms altho' the windows were only open a little way. A house was blown down at Clapham and it even stopped Big Ben!" *(29 December 1914)*

"London is absolutely the same with the exception of darkness at nights, which hurts no-one. Restaurants are just as crowded at lunch – in fact the City is every bit the same. As for Muswell Hill, you would never know we are at war up there." *(29 December 1914)*

"There has been a good deal of spotted fever about. I don't know about the front, but they have had it in England, nearly everywhere where soldiers are and it is almost always fatal. A young girl caught it at Stroud Green and died and you remember my speaking of the Richardsons - his brother also died from it, but he was not in the army. Ernie said about 16 were buried at Eastertime with it and they also had it at Crystal Palace where the Naval Reservists are."

"We had dinner up west, feeling desperate and inclined for anything. They had an orchestra of 3 – all young fellows. It was French Flag Night and they started off with the Marseillaise, whereupon we all had to stand up amidst much cheering and clapping – we were glad we had got through our first course otherwise we should not have been able to take our noses off our plates, as it was we cast longing eyes at the sweets and devotedly hoped no more national anthems were coming." *(18 July 1915)*

"I am not looking forward to this winter – everywhere is so dark – stations so murky you can't distinguish friend from foe. Carriages so dark you can't see to read – streets positively dangerous as it is difficult to tell the speed of the vehicles in the gloom. The only thing to do is to get home as early as possible and tuck oneself in for the night." *(19 October 1916)*

"Hilda and I couldn't see one another going down Colney Hatch Lane, it was only her white collar which showed me where she was – of course, this is all down to the new lighting regulations, earlier closing of shops, etc. I am dreading the winter, it will be a gloomy time in every way – still, it's all for our safety, so we can't grumble and get fed up, besides, we have all of us got to suffer something and this won't be much, if it's the worst we have to encounter." *(18 October 1916)*

"On Saturday we had the worst fog since 1902. Win and I had gone to Louie's to tea intending to leave early, but it was all we could do to find their house and as it came on worse we had to stick there – all buses and traffic generally was stopped. E. left town at 2.40pm by train and arrived at Highgate Station at 5 o'clock. Cheers! I do like living in England!" *(19 December 1916)*

"I am not looking forward to the dark winter nights. Lighting regulations are terribly strict now and not a glimmer must show through windows, so we have to shade our lights and hang dark curtains up. One man, who just returned to his house from the Front, threw open a window to get some air - the wind blew the curtains and he was fined £1. This, and several other instances, was in the "Evening News" tonight. Rather a shame when only an accident, but it shows how careful we have got to be. We shall all develop into cats and begin to see in the dark." *(17 September 1916)*

"It is very difficult now for foreigners to leave London – they have to go to a police station, have passports and fill a book up with particulars – a family history in fact." *(22 September 1916)*

"Sunday night, to try and cheer ourselves up, we all went down to Finsbury Park to a concert which was quite good but it took us 1½ hours to get home, owing to a bus breaking down on the hill – quite exciting. We were shot about in all directions and finally had to get out. The funny part was there was another stranded a few yards from ours – no signs of a driver, conductor or passengers. I suppose they had left in disgust." *(21 February 1917)*

"I had an adventure on Sunday night, going home from Rees. Buses were taken off for some reason or other and I was at Highgate waiting for one. I waited and waited and at last took a train to East Finchley in order to walk (no trains to Muswell Hill on Sundays) but it was so dark and lonely and I could hear the Belgian guns in the distance and it fairly put the wind up. When I got to the police station up Fortis Green I was in a fair funk. There were two special constables there so more as an excuse than anything else I asked if there were any more buses. Of course, they said "No" and asked where I wanted to go and told me the best way was down Tetherdown. I said "No thanks, not at this time of night, I'm too nervous." So one said if you wait two ticks I shall be off duty and will see you home if you will permit me to do so. I was in too much alarm, so I gratefully accepted and arrived home "in the arms of the law" at 12.15." *(25 July 1917)*

A B-type bus passes Muswell Hill Station after a long climb up Muswell Hill
(Capital Transport)

As the war progressed, conditions for those left at home grew steadily worse and the cost of living rose alarmingly as Mabel pointed out:

> "From what I can see you ought to stand a chance of getting something decent to do when you get back. There are plenty of positions going now, but of course they may fill up quickly when the war is over." *(23 February 1915)*

> "The Separation Allowance for a sergeant is now 15/- and I might have saved about £20." *(7 April 1915)*

> "And now for a piece of news – I had a rise today to £2 a week!" *(26 May 1915)*

> "There is one problem I think and one which may end us in civil war – these strikers and also the overpaid wives of soldiers – women and men who perhaps only got 18/- a week between them, now get anything from 25/- to 30/- a week and more. Is it likely they are

going back to their former wage!! Also look at the coal strike – thousands out at a time like this. They applied the new Strike Act, which the men defied and then Lloyd George goes to Cardiff and settles the strike by giving them all they want!! We shall be absolutely in the hands of these wretches ere long." *(27 July 1915)*

"The new Budget is out - taxes getting worse and worse. A sovereign is now worth about one third and Uncle E says it means another £1000 off his income. The halfpenny post is abolished – not that that is any hardship. Tea will be 2/3d a pound. A man earning £600 will be only worth about £300. I suppose things will get worse." *(23 September 1915)*

"You won't get kippers floating in butter when you come back – we happen to be at war too and I expect you will get the "kips" minus butter!! *(8 November 1915)*

"The pictures are still open but I'm afraid it will have to be the 3d seats if this war lasts much longer. I have never been so hard up before – it does make a difference, as everything has gone up in price. It makes you wonder what conditions must be like in Germany. We shall be the next to want the workhouse." *(22 November 1915)*

"As for prices, they are worse every day. We have to pay quite double for our lunches to say nothing of clothes etc – everything, in fact. It is these people who have small fixed incomes who are the real sufferers, others who are nursing large war profits, do not feel the pinch so much. I suppose we must be thankful that we can live at all in these dreadful times but what a relief it will be when it's all over." *(22 November 1916)*

"After lunch today I had three biscuits and a cup of coffee, for which the charge is 5d – 2½d for three biscuits! In some places coffee is 3d – 4d a cup." *(4 December 1916)*

"I didn't go out after all on Sunday, as a new order came into force the day before prohibiting cars being hired for pleasure." *(25 May 1917)*

"Things are awfully miserable and I am sick of this beastly struggle for existence. We have none of Gerald's affairs settled yet can get hardly anything for mother. I have been having a lot of trouble again on this. The only people who are treated well are the wives – other dependents get practically nothing, in spite of what one reads in the papers. What they say is not carried out and it is only when you get up against them that one discovers this – it is all very cruel. Why should a young married girl (sometimes a "bit") get a jolly good pension without any trouble and is besides still earning for herself a good salary, and someone in mother's position, not able to do anything, cannot get even a tiny pension. It is very unjust and only makes me angry. It is worthwhile being married, I can see why there are so many weddings." *(24 July 1918)*

As time progressed, Mabel's letters reflected her changing attitudes to the war:

"You will see from "The Times" Gen. French's report in which he says: "Hold on for a little longer and you will be chasing a beaten enemy." This was to the troops so it sounds hopeful." *(21 September 1914)*

"The news, although good, seems to point to a long war." *(21 September 1914)*

"I do wish it would end – it's too awful. You cannot imagine how depressed I get at times, and think of the hundreds of thousands of our brave men simply being slaughtered. I say, it's wicked and should never have been allowed." *(27 October 1914)*

"I've heard from very good sources that the war will soon be over and that we are to have big events shortly. This is the first and I should say that they have lured the Germans out so as to have a big sea fight just at the time when they are in a bad way on land." *(11 December 1914)*

"The tone in the City is decidedly cheerful and I cannot help feeling things are going well – some say it will be soon over, but I'm afraid to think of such good news." *(8 January 1915)*

"This war makes me so disgusted. I really haven't patience to write about it! It should never have happened and is too wicked for anything." *(12 January 1915)*

"As for the war, I'm sick of it – England's not worth fighting for in my opinion – men striking and haggling over extra pay while the best men are giving their lives. The strikers are hanging up everything, shipping and munitions. A deputation waited on the Chancellor on Monday and it now looks as if drink will be prohibited altogether. The whole war is wicked and simply a slaughter of valuable lives for nothing. Don't talk to me of patriotism – it's everyone for themselves now, I don't see the use of saving England from the Germans just for a parcel of socialistic money grabbers and foreigners." *(29 March 1915)*

"Everyone seems to think the war is going to last 2 years now." *(21 May 1915)*

"We certainly are in a serious position – what with Romania failing, sinking of ships etc. etc. and now political crisis. Lloyd George resigned, Asquith resigned etc. etc, I wonder what is going to happen to us all. I can tell you everyone is <u>far from</u> cheerful." *(4 December 1916)*

"You say why don't I invest in War Bonds – I wouldn't touch anything to do with WAR with the end of a poker." *(18 March 1918)*

Mabel's younger brother Gerald had applied for and was eventually accepted in the Royal Flying Corps. He became a pilot and was sent to France where, along with others, was involved in actions above the front lines. On Gerald's visits home on leave he would hire a motor car and take Mabel and her sister Win on trips to the country and they would also visit theatres and cinemas.

Mabel's mother had always been worried that Gerald had decided he wanted to fly, doubtless because of the reports in the press of the many accidents that were occurring due to inexperienced pilots and the primitive and unreliable aircraft. On 25 September 1917 Mabel sent Lionel a telegram:

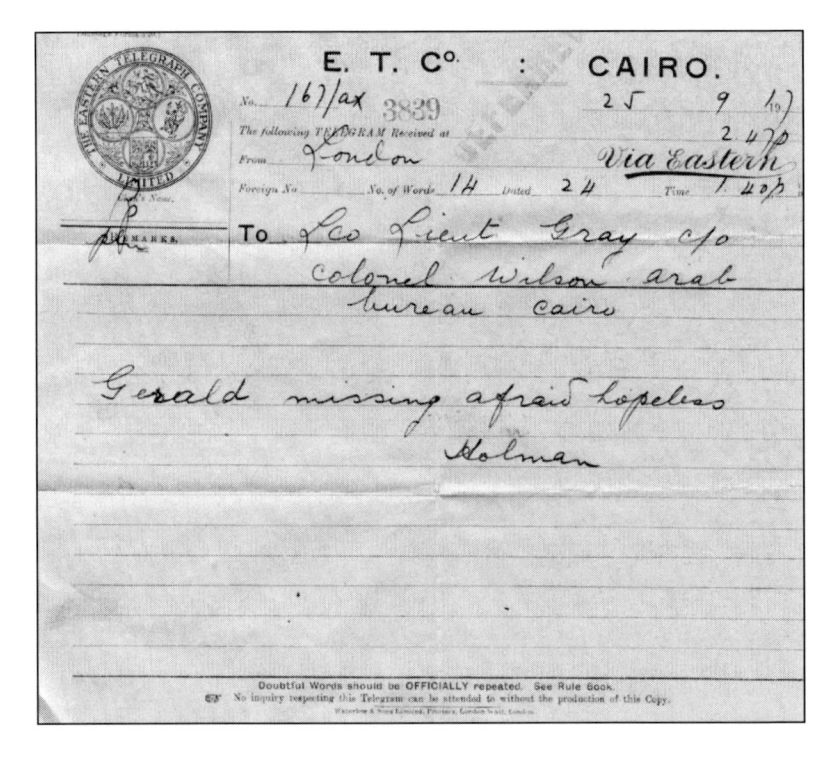

This followed from a letter that had been received by Mabel's mother and which confirmed her worst fears.

                                    41st Squadron, R.F.C.

                       18th September 1917

Dear Mrs Holman,

          It is with very great regret that I have to inform you that your son, Lieutenant G. C. Holman, was brought down by a German Pilot while on Patrol yesterday morning at 7,20a.m. about 7 miles due E. of Arras.
          He was leading a Patrol of three machines from this squadron when he sighted three German machines, which, according to the description and colour of their machines, were Pilots belonging to the famous German "Circus."
          Your son immediately attacked them.
          During the fight which followed (from what I can gather from eye witnesses) the leading German got behind your son and opened fire at short range, when the right wing of his machine was seen to fold back and he fell to earth behind the German lines.
          The German machine was eventually brought down by a machine of our Patrol.
          There is a chance that your Boy was not killed, but those who saw the fight hold out no hope.
          I have known Lieutenant Holman for two months and a more popular man in a squadron it would be hard to imagine.
          He died as we are all sure he would liked to have died, leading his Patrol into action.
          I will forward at once any information I may receive which, please God, will be hopful for us all.
          I need hardly say that his loss to the Squadron is keenly felt by his Brother Officers who join with me in desiring to give expression to our deep sympathy with your bereavement.
          Believe me to be.
                    Yours very sincerely

                              F. Powell
                              Major

Commanding
     41st Squadron, R.F.C.

On 30 September she was able to give more details:

> "To make matters more agonising he was due home in a few days! He wasn't really fit for flying and when we asked him to stay here for treatment he said: "I can't let the other fellows down." You see they were all new to the game and Gerald was evidently their best man. It's too awful, we have spent an agonizing week and I cannot think of the future at all – there seems nothing left to live for – he was our all and the loveliest youngster. Everyone loved him."

```
                                    13th Wing,
                                       R.F.C.
                                 September 19th, 1917.

Dear Mrs Holman,

            You will have received by now the news that your
Son was reported "missing" on September 17th, and that,
from all this evidence that can be gathered, there is
little chance of his having escaped death.
            I want to send you my very deepest sympathy – of
course there is still the very small hope remaining that
news may yet come through that he managed to land on the
other side of the lines and that he is a prisoner, but in
this case it is so slight that you must not build on it.
            Your Son was a particular friend of mine – we
used to do a good many things together from time to time
whenever I lived with 41 squadron. We bathed together,
played chess, and talked a lot of nonsense, such as one
does talk out here. His loss is a very serious one for the
squadron – for he had the name of being one of their
stoutest Pilots. I remember standing in the Aerodrome once
when one of their Patrols was going up. One machine was in
obvious difficulties with its Engine, which was misfiring
badly. I asked a Mechanic who was standing by whether the
Pilot oughtn't to bring it back at once and he said that
most of them would but if it was Mr. Holman he would
probably stick it out and try and keep with the Patrol.
That is very high praise indeed – it is a nasty thing to
stunt over the lines with an engine that may fail any
minute. In time it will be a comfort to you to think of
things like that – of the courage and self-sacrifice of
such a life and death; but at first it will be difficult
for you to think of the future at all – may God give you
strength and help.

            With my most sincere sympathy.

                  I remain,

                        Yours very truly.

                        R.W.Dugdale

                        (Chaplain)
```

A letter was to follow from one of Gerald's comrades:

> September 20th, 1917
>
> Dear Madam,
>
> I hope you will pardon me for taking the liberty to write to you, but having been the late Mr G. C. Holman's Batman for the last 8 months I felt I must express my deepest sympathy to you and family in your trouble. I miss him very much, he was such a "Sport" and a Gentleman in every way and missed by everyone, both Mechanics and Officers. Several days ago he asked for and received my Photo, and promised to send one of his to my private address viz: 39 Cromer Road, Tooting Junction, London S.W. 17, so would be very much obliged if you would kindly favour me with one. I have packed his kit and should anything not be correct I would be very pleased to supply you with particulars of same.
>
> I remain,
>
> Yours sincerely,
>
> (2/A.M.) J. H. Sansom

On 13 October 1917 Mabel wrote to Lionel:

> "I can't write more, my heart is too full of our dear old Gerald. Some day I may be able to write you a better letter and give more details but at present it is impossible. I can't give my mind to anything, but I know you will understand – I think of you always, but everything seems unreal now. We can't get a proper aspect of anything and certainly cannot believe we shall never see the dear again."

Mabel's letters contained many references to her disappointment that they had not got married before Lionel had left for Egypt, but her wish did not come true until two years after the end of the war. They were married in

Alexandria on 20 November 1920, but she was unable to cope with the climate and they returned to England in 1922.

Lionel, who by then had reached the rank of Captain, resigned from the services and, being by then an expert in radio, considered the commercial possibilities of wireless so he approached the Marconi Company who were the first in the field with apparatus and they suggested that he open a depot with their support and good will. He selected a shop on Muswell Hill Broadway and was the first man in the country to become a Marconiphone dealer. Mabel and William had two children. She died in 1948 and he died in 1963 and his son, Gerald, carried on the business until the 1970s when increasing competition from multiples made them uncompetitive.

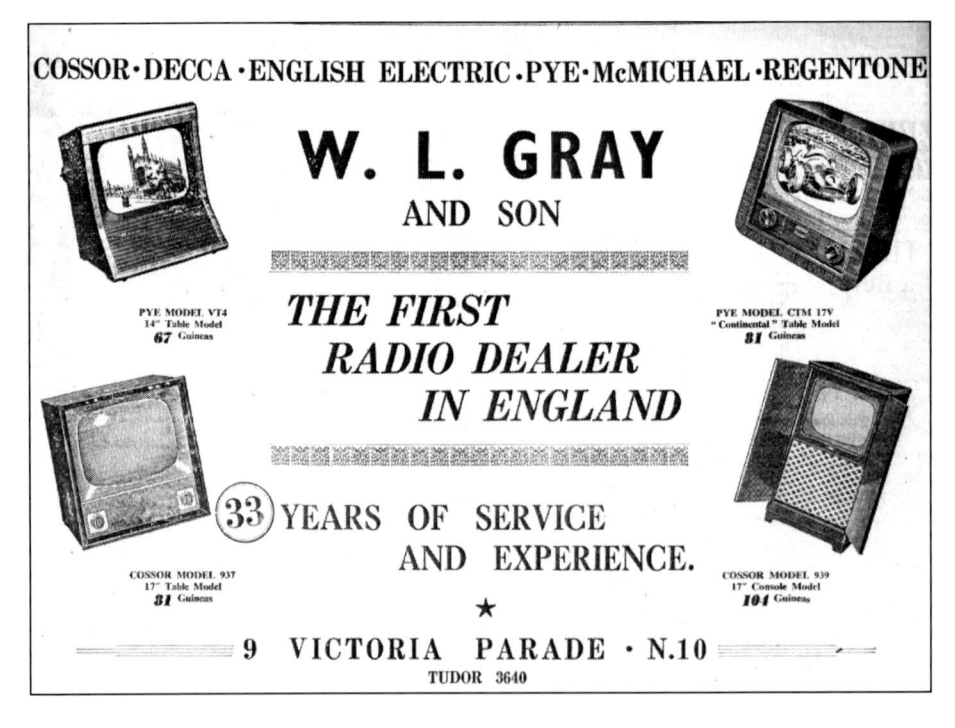

An advertisement in "Muswell Hill Record" of 18 February 1956

CHAPTER 6

SEND MORE MEN

By the early part of 1915 as the realities of the war began to sink in, the number of volunteers started to drop significantly. The *Barnet Press* published the following:

SEND ALONG THE NAMES.

We want to compile a list of all Local Men in the districts served by the *Barnet Press* who are serving their Country in the present crisis. The list will be interesting to readers generally, and as a record should be valuable.

We therefore invite Parents and Friends of Men on Service to send us the names. A Postcard will suffice. For example:—

JOHN TOWNSEND, Holly Park,
    Friern Barnet (7th Middx. Regt.).

EDWARD SHORT, Market-place,
    East Finchley (H.M.S. Dreadnought).

(*'Barnet Press'* 27 March 1915)

Every week thereafter the paper would publish long lists of men from the area who had enlisted. Another column, the "Roll of Honour", gave the names of those killed and was added to every week. The paper also ran "War Notes" which included such items as "Barnet special constables are no longer doing duty on the Parish Church tower. It is understood that men of the anti-aircraft corps will keep watch on the tower in the future" and "Mr Hood of Friern Barnet Grammar School, was presented with a wrist watch, pipe and pouch by the master and boys of the school on his joining the Artists' Rifles."

Pressure on local men to volunteer was great. In February 1915 a Battalion parade of 600-700 men of the Finchley, Friern Barnet and New Southgate Training Corps was held in Friary Park and prompted the question in the press "How can I stand off and not do my part, when these men are doing theirs? Come along and play the man; join the training corps and do your bit; don't be a slacker." And "A man's duty is now plainly set before him. If he cannot enlist it is his duty to join the Corps. The need is great."

In April 1915 the *Barnet Press* reported that there was a big crowd at a recruiting fete organised by the New Southgate Company of the Finchley, Friern Barnet and New Southgate Battalion of the Middlesex Volunteer Regiment which was held at the Recreation Ground in New Southgate. Estimates of the number attending varied; the police thought there were 2000 there, the groundsman thought 3000 and the secretary estimated 4000. Whatever the figure, the event included tug-of-war, marching in quick time, slow marching as well as series of races.

A series of advertisements was run which were designed to shame people into joining up.

Pressure was also put on employers; the National Organising Committee for War Savings condemned "selfish, thoughtless extravagance of families who kept chauffeurs, and used cars and motor cycles for pleasure."

DO YOU FEEL HAPPY?

Do you feel happy as you walk along the streets and see other men wearing the King's uniform?

If not, why don't you enlist to-day and do your share?

('Barnet Press' 6 February 1915)

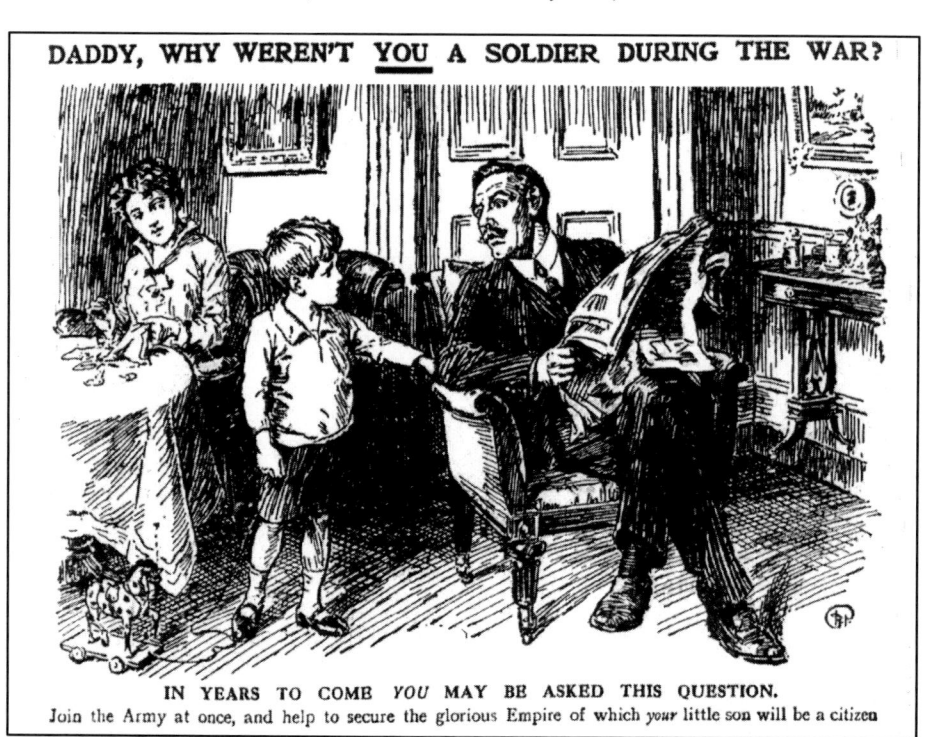

DADDY, WHY WEREN'T YOU A SOLDIER DURING THE WAR?

IN YEARS TO COME YOU MAY BE ASKED THIS QUESTION.
Join the Army at once, and help to secure the glorious Empire of which your little son will be a citizen

('Barnet Press' 27 February 1915)

('Barnet Press' 13 February 1915)

('Barnet Press' 20 February 1915)

Appeals were made to both men and women. In the *Barnet Press* of 6 March 1915:

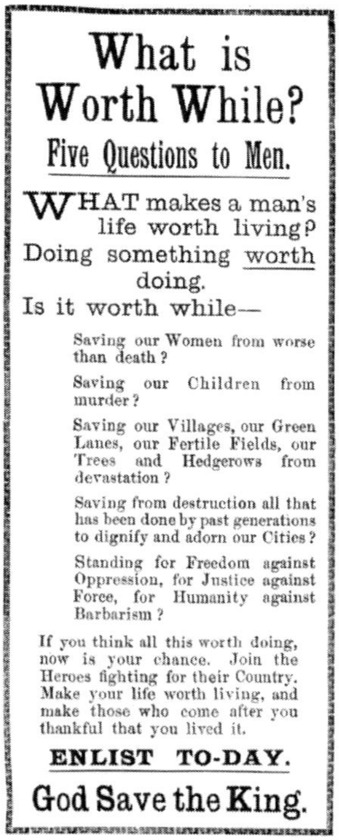

What is Worth While?
Five Questions to Men.

WHAT makes a man's life worth living? Doing something worth doing. Is it worth while—

Saving our Women from worse than death?

Saving our Children from murder?

Saving our Villages, our Green Lanes, our Fertile Fields, our Trees and Hedgerows from devastation?

Saving from destruction all that has been done by past generations to dignify and adorn our Cities?

Standing for Freedom against Oppression, for Justice against Force, for Humanity against Barbarism?

If you think all this worth doing, now is your chance. Join the Heroes fighting for their Country. Make your life worth living, and make those who come after you thankful that you lived it.

ENLIST TO-DAY.
God Save the King.

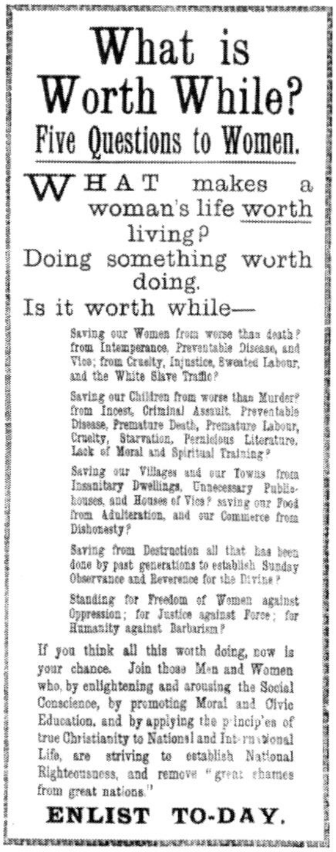

What is Worth While?
Five Questions to Women.

WHAT makes a woman's life worth living? Doing something worth doing. Is it worth while—

Saving our Women from worse than death? from Intemperance, Preventable Disease, and Vice; from Cruelty, Injustice, Sweated Labour, and the White Slave Traffic?

Saving our Children from worse than Murder? from Incest, Criminal Assault, Preventable Disease, Premature Death, Premature Labour, Cruelty, Starvation, Pernicious Literature, Lack of Moral and Spiritual Training?

Saving our Villages and our Towns from Insanitary Dwellings, Unnecessary Public-houses, and Houses of Vice? saving our Food from Adulteration, and our Commerce from Dishonesty?

Saving from Destruction all that has been done by past generations to establish Sunday Observance and Reverence for the Divine?

Standing for Freedom of Women against Oppression; for Justice against Force; for Humanity against Barbarism?

If you think all this worth doing, now is your chance. Join those Men and Women who, by enlightening and arousing the Social Conscience, by promoting Moral and Civic Education, and by applying the principles of true Christianity to National and International Life, are striving to establish National Righteousness, and remove "great shames from great nations."

ENLIST TO-DAY.

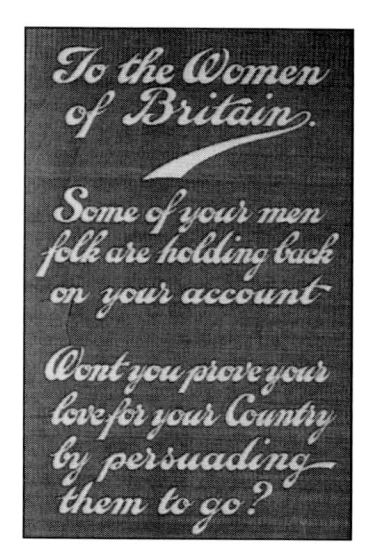

To the Women of Britain

Some of your men folk are holding back on your account

Wont you prove your love for your Country by persuading them to go?

THERE'S ROOM FOR YOU

ENLIST TO-DAY

(©IWM Art.IWM PST 4884) 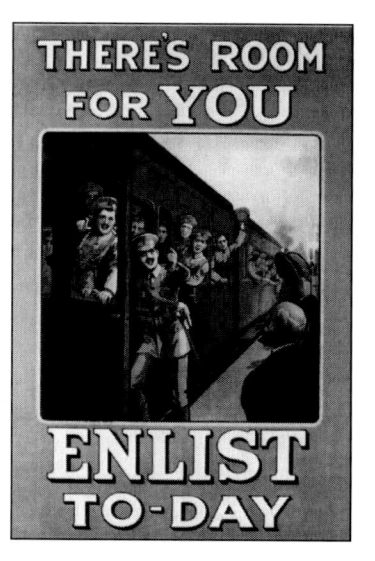   (©IWM.IWM PST 12246)

A series of posters was issued with such slogans as "Who's Absent – is it You?" and, aimed at women, "Women of Britain, say 'Go'" and "Is your best boy wearing khaki? Don't you think he should be?" and "If your young man neglects his duty to King and Country, the time may come when he will neglect you."

One of the enduring stories from the Home Front is of women presenting white feathers to men on the streets – a sign of cowardice – in an attempt to get them to enlist. This letter to the editor from April 1915 gives a man's point of view: "I have recently received an unsigned typewritten note, posted locally, suggesting that I should enlist and that I am at present living "the life of a coward." There is no address inside; the address on the envelope is a good hand – I think female. One cannot answer such a letter in the ordinary way, hence this letter to you. And I should be interested to hear whether this impertinence is general or not.

Who could resist the call to arms?   *(©IWM Art.IWM PST 5086)*

Assuming that the sender is of the female sex – if not, I owe the sex an apology – and that mine is not an isolated instance, I should like to ask: Does this person imagine that the recipients of her favour have not already given the question the grave consideration which it obviously deserves? Would she not admit that it is a question which every man must settle for himself? If so, what right has she to question the correctness of the decision? Presumably the man in question knows more about his affairs than she does. In any case, does she imagine that she will get a single recruit by such methods? I wonder if such persons ever stop to think that they may be intruding not only upon a man's private affairs, but also upon his most sacred sorrows. It may well be that the recipient has done his best to go, but, being in a bank, has not had the good fortune to draw a winning number in the lottery as to which of the bank's employees should go; it may be that he is running business at a loss in order to keep a score or so of men at work, thus saving them and their families from destitution; it may be that he is giving up valuable time during the day to Red Cross or Belgian refugee work, and also perhaps much-needed hours of rest to the dreary but necessary duties of the special constabulary. Are these persons so dense that they cannot see that there are many ways of serving – aye, and royally serving – our King and country in these critical times? Many who at present cannot enlist might do so, if it were not that it would mean leaving liabilities and obligations to fall upon shoulders which are unable to bear them. In such a case a man must have the courage, not to go, but to stay. He may have excellent reasons for thus deciding the great question – which he would be willing to give to anyone who has the right to ask for them, but not to a person who has not the courage to put either name or address to a charge of cowardice. Till she does so, I shall simply sign myself – Yours etc. X.Y.Z."

In one week in February 1915 some 43 names were listed. Perhaps it was the latter idea, together with reports from the Front of the conditions that slowed down recruitment throughout the country. The Government appointed a Director of Recruiting, Lord Derby, in 1915 and in July of that year the National Registration Act was passed which required every citizen between the ages of 15 and 65 to register their name, place of residence and nature of work. Three months later it had been established that there were 5,185,211 men of military age and of these there were still 3,400,000 who qualified for military service but had not yet joined up.

Mabel Holman commented on enlistment:

> "This morning we had a government notice asking who there was in the household, if eligible and willing to join – a form of conscription from war office and every householder is receiving it." *(3 December 1914)*

> "Kitchener in his speech in the House did not ask for more men, in spite of all the bosh the papers put in – they make me wild. I think they have as many men as they want - and can clothe. Herbert Godwin joined Kitchener's Army at the starting of the war and had not got his uniform at Xmas!" *(8 January 1915)*

> "The National Register is next thing for voluntary service and all between 16 and 61 are asked to go – They are going to start on women next." *(8 February 1917)*

A letter in the *Barnet Press* of 27 February 1915 from Lance Sergeant Rusted of Potters Bar gave a good description of the training that new recruits would have to go through:

> "I wonder if the ordinary stay-at-home youth who only leaves his home when he takes his annual holiday, and even then only for a short time, realises how narrow-minded the force of circumstances which usually exist in times of peace make him. Personally, previous to joining the Army, I had only a very hazy idea of what a soldier's training consisted of. It used to be a generally accepted maxim that if a man was a failure in every other walk of life he stood an excellent chance of making a good soldier. 'He has only to

practice shooting and do as he is told,' was the argument. A careful scrutiny of the reports of 'Tommy' at the Front, and a few days or even a few hours spent with the recruits at home, will soon silence the argument. Haven't repeated occurrences at the Front, where an officer has been put out of action, and some 'ranker' has immediately taken over control with every success, proved that 'Tommy' is taught to think for himself? And that is where he scores over the poor German soldier, who is not allowed to 'think.' The Army makes a man self-reliant, improves his health, and broadens his mind by travel and experience to an almost incredible extent.

Just a short survey of those things which go to make up a soldier's training may not be out of place here. First of all, a recruit is taught the rudiments of ordinary squad drill. But don't imagine the teaching to 'right turn' or 'left turn' is the only object of this elementary stage. It teaches a man to be alert, always to obey the least command of a superior, and to work harmoniously with his comrades. The moral effect is really greater than the practical. Our recruit is next taught to drill with a rifle, which gives him a feeling of security and teaches him to use his rifle as though it was part and parcel of him – an extra limb provided by the Government to equip him against the extra perils he has to face.

Next, he is taught the first stages of musketry, and fires his grouping practice on a miniature range. Then follows bayonet fighting, additional musketry, company training, battalion training under the supervision of the colonel himself, divisional training carried out under the supervision of an awe-inspiring personage who is designated a general. In conjunction with the two latter stages of training, mock battles are waged in which blank ammunition is used. The somewhat intricate yet perfect method of protecting a large body of troops which is advancing through an enemy's country by detaching an advance guard must be learned too. Sentry work and outpost duty are also to be practised extensively.

To come back to the doings of the particular battalion to which I belong. We were sent from the depot at Chester to a small village called Codford, which is on the borders of Salisbury Plain and about fourteen miles from the town of Salisbury itself. At this small village we spent eight or nine weeks under canvas. About the end of October, however, continual heavy rains and the constant tramping of thousands of troops on the training grounds soon reduced the place to a tremendous quagmire, and made it quite unfit for further training. Early in November we transferred to billets in Bournemouth, and I can honestly say that at this popular holiday resort we spent some of the happiest days of our life. The billets were excellent and the food was of the best quality. The people of Bournemouth welcomed us and did all that was in their power to give us a good time. Eleven happy weeks we spent in Bournemouth, and then we were again transferred to Codford. It was a big change, but everything had been done at Codford by a pioneer battalion to make us comfortable. We are now living in huts, which are a perfect protection against inclement weather. Improvised tables are fitted up, and each man is now supplied with a straw mattress, which fits upon three planks (raised from the floor by means of small trestles), and three blankets. The food is excellent, and there is plenty if it. Unfortunately the mud is still with us, but, still, that cannot be helped. Training still goes on steadily. First parade 7 to 8; second parade 9 to 1; afternoon parade 2 to 5; night parades are not uncommon, while lectures are given to the various Companies about three times a week, and take up about an hour."

By December 1915 there were still 2 million men who had not volunteered so in January 1916 the Government passed the Military Service Act which introduced conscription for all fit unmarried men and widowers between the ages of eighteen and forty-one. Exceptions were made for those suffering from ill health, and Local Tribunals were set up to hear appeals against the call up by men who claimed exemption on a number of grounds – if their business would suffer serious hardship; if they were doing work of national importance or if they had a conscientious objection to doing combatant service. The rulings of the Local Tribunals appeared in the *Barnet Press*. Here are a few of them:

- Sidney Turner of 17 Parkhurst Road, a clerk on the G.N. Railway. The ground claim was that the appellant was the sole support of the home and his widowed mother. Appeal granted.
- Charles Hart, Glenthorne Road, greengrocer. Main supporter of widowed mother. Applied for exemption some weeks ago. Refused.
- Alfred Colman of 106 Holly Park Road, in the employment of Mr Vincent of 57 Friern Barnet-road. The employer said that Mr Colman was a slaughterer, and was the only man available for the work. Exemption granted for three months.
- William Sanders of 52 Cromwell Road, a "butcher in all its branches" and a support of widowed mother. It was reported that in the family there were five brothers, eligible for the Army, and that four were appealing. Refused.

Military Service Act, 1916.

THE following is an extract from a Minute of the London Yearly Meeting of the Society of Friends held specially from January 28th to 30th last:—

"We feel that Friends will have a duty in watching the action of the Tribunals, in giving advice to young men with regard to the statement of their conscientious objections before these Tribunals, including, if necessary, the Appeal Tribunals.

"We decide also to make known our readiness to advise conscientious objectors other than Friends so far as is in our power."

Any interested are invited to enter into communication with
E. C. MORLAND,
Leith Hill, Whetstone.

Quakers were among the conscientious objectors. ('Barnet Press' 26 February 1916)

- Albert E Dymoke, in the employment of a firm of house furnishers, residing at Eastern Cottage, East Road, New Southgate. Business hardship. Answering the Chairman, the appellant said that he had been in the Army for 21 years. He joined the Army as a trumpeter when he was 14 years of age. He contended that under the terms of his discharge he was liable to be called up for service in the United Kingdom. That meant that he was still a soldier, and did not come within the scope of the Military Service Act – the case was referred to the War Office.
- Hubert A Smith, carter, of 3 Bawtry-road, Oakleigh-road. Business hardship. Exempted as long as the appellant continues his present occupation.

A case featuring a conscientious objector (C.O.) appeared in the 13 May issue of the *Barnet Press*:

> "Horace Gates of 56, Wilton Road. – The appellant, an objector to service, asked the Court to review his case on the ground that since the Court had dealt with it, occupations of a kind more suited to his temperament had been placed on the list of services into which objectors could be drafted. The Chairman said that the appellant, when he first appeared, based his claim for exemption on conscientious grounds and he was exempted from combatant service. He appealed to the Middlesex Tribunal against the decision of the Friern Barnet Court, and the appeal was dismissed. The appellant now asked the Friern Barnet Court to certify him for one of the civil occupations of national importance recommended by the Parliamentary Committee as suited for men of his temperament. Mr Bell (military representative) contended that as the appeal had been settled it was *ultra vires* for the Friern Barnet Court to consider the application for review. Mr Barfield (chairman) read the Regulations, and said that according to these the appellant was within his rights in making this application but before the Court went into the details of the case again the appellant would have to put forward substantial reasons for review. Mr Bell said that if men could make application

after application for review, on a different ground every time, the men needed for the Army would never be obtained. Mr Barfield said that the Court was bound by Regulation to which they would adhere. After hearing the appellant, the Court decided to review the case."

It is clear from this that conscientious objectors did not attract a lot of support. *The Barnet Press* reported on 27 May 1915: "We understand that several of the Finchley Council's clerical staff have threatened to go on strike if "conscientious objectors" to combatant service are allowed to take the places of their colleagues who have joined the colours. Good!"

> **THE CONSCIENTIOUS OBJECTOR AT THE FRONT!**
>
> OH, YOU NAUGHTY UNKIND GERMAN —
> REALLY, IF YOU DON'T DESIST
> I'LL FORGET I'VE GOT A CONSCIENCE,
> AND I'LL SMACK YOU ON THE WRIST!

C.O.s were offered the opportunity to join a Non-Combatant Corps in the Army or to work on farms, in forestry or other manual jobs which would help the war effort. Some 6000 of those who refused to do any of these were imprisoned. The war also started to affect everyday life as can be seen from this on 6 February 1915:

> "The teachers in the schools of Southgate and Friern Barnet have certainly not been found wanting in the country's hour of need, for twenty of them – in fact, nearly all of military age – are now serving in the colours, three as lieutenants, and several as non-coms. Their expert knowledge of the Swedish drill now taught in all the schools secured for them rapid promotion. Lieutenant C Daniels of St Paul's School, New Southgate, has been in charge of his Company in the trenches for several weeks; many of the others are also in foreign service. The lady teachers are making woollen articles, and from each school large consignments of knitted goods have been forwarded to our brave fighting men on land and sea. The boys in one school provided a grand supply of wool. The girls had promised to knit as much as wool as the boys provided. This was incidentally the cause of the sudden shrinkage in the receipts of the neighbouring tuck shops. The teachers have subscribed upwards of £50 to the Prince of Wales Relief Fund, and the money has been forwarded, per the local relief funds of Southgate and Friern Barnet. In addition the teachers have, with the aid of friends, furnished a Belgian refugee home at 63 Friern Barnet Road and are now supporting a family (Mr and Mrs Van Dyck and children) consisting of nine adults. The only son of military age has after some three weeks of training been rejected by the Belgian Army on medical grounds."

A letter from Sydney J.R. Bennett of 2 Waterworks-cottages, North Finchley in the 16 January 1916 issue of *Barnet Press* under the heading "Come On, Finchley! Come On, Barnet!" highlighted the problem of recruitment. Mr Bennett was apparently in the Royal Army Medical Corps in Belgium but his letter could almost have been written by the army public relations department:

> "According to our local roll we don't seem to be doing great things our way in the matter of recruiting, and from what I can see we only

get men recruiting who already have members of their family serving – for instance, the Bentleys, Soars, and Mastersons. Now there are plenty of other young men of recruitable age round about our district who want bucking up. Now, come on Finchley. Set an example. We can do this easily enough, but we must have men to relieve the tired ones – not tired of fighting, but physically tired.

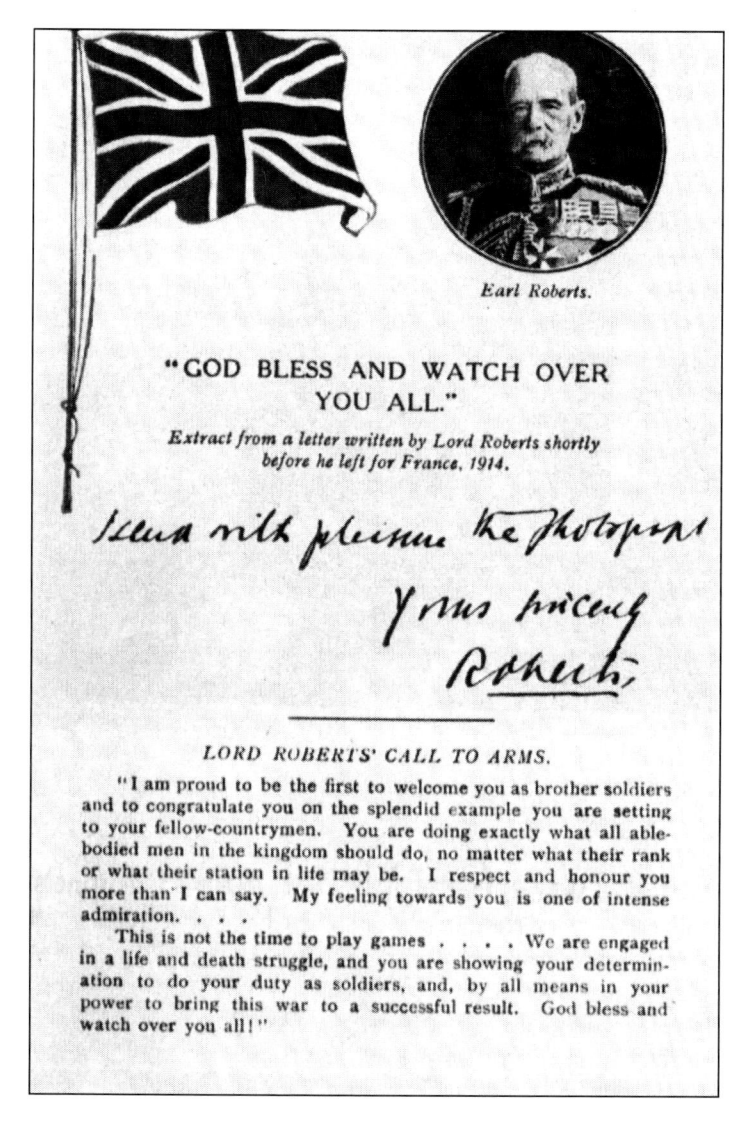

Earl Roberts.

"GOD BLESS AND WATCH OVER YOU ALL."

Extract from a letter written by Lord Roberts shortly before he left for France, 1914.

LORD ROBERTS' CALL TO ARMS.

"I am proud to be the first to welcome you as brother soldiers and to congratulate you on the splendid example you are setting to your fellow-countrymen. You are doing exactly what all able-bodied men in the kingdom should do, no matter what their rank or what their station in life may be. I respect and honour you more than I can say. My feeling towards you is one of intense admiration. . . .

This is not the time to play games . . . . We are engaged in a life and death struggle, and you are showing your determination to do your duty as soldiers, and, by all means in your power to bring this war to a successful result. God bless and watch over you all!"

Welcome to the army

Now let's see that roll get longer each week. A good life, a hard life, and all the boys out here. 'Funk holes' are near the fighting line, not near our district, I hope. Plenty have shouted 'Come on Finchley!' 'Come on Barnet' at football on Saturdays. Now the country calls, let's see the response. Come on Finchley! Come on Barnet! Now set an example. Everything merry and bright out here, bar weather. Good luck to the 'Barnet Press.'"

MEN IN ARMS

Who Hail from "Barnet Press" Area

THIRTY-SEVENTH LIST.

[We shall be pleased to publish names as they reach us.]

BARNET.

KING, H. S., 13, Dollis-cottages, Totteridge-lane, 3/7th Middlesex, Reigate.

POULTON, TOM, 71, Puller-road, Barnet, Herts Territorials, Hertford.

FINCHLEY & WHETSTONE

BABB, SYDNEY, 55, Station-road, Church End, Finchley, R.A.M.C.

CLARIDGE, A. J. R., 4, Oakleigh-road, Whetstone, N . 6th City of London Rifles (T.F.), British Expeditionary Force.

COY, GEORGE, 3, Oxley-villas, Bulwer-road, New Barnet, East Kent Mounted Rifles, Canterbury.

HULBERT, THOMAS G., 7, Sunnyside, Swan-lane, Whetstone, 6th Battalion Middlesex Regiment.

SMITH, PERCY JAMES, 16, Queen s-avenue, Whetstone, A.S.C., Motor Transport, British Expeditionary Force.

NEW SOUTHGATE

HYDE, DRIVER W. E. 69, Cromwell-road, New Southgate, Heavy Battery, R F A

WALKER, A. WILLIAM, 134, Palmers-road, New Southgate, Military Mounted Police, 47th (London) Division, T.F

CHAPTER 7

THE COST OF THE WAR

The economic cost of a long war fought on several fronts was obviously going to put a severe strain on Britain and the lights in Whitehall must have been burning throughout the night as civil servants calculated how they were going to raise money to pay for it. Britain had inherited a strong economy from the Victorians but even this would not be enough to finance the purchase of munitions, the equipping, supplying and paying a large army and navy, and the increased cost of imports. Three options were available – raiding existing reserves, borrowing money from home and abroad or raising taxes at home. The Government adopted all three.

As early as two days after the declaration of war Parliament voted for a sum of £100 million but this was only an initial calculation and in his first Budget in November 1914 David Lloyd George doubled the rate of income tax to 1/6d in the pound. It was estimated then that war was costing £1 million a day; by May 1915 the daily cost had risen to £2.1 million.

Not surprisingly, costs continued to escalate and by September 1915 the daily cost of the war had risen to £3.5 million. The Budget in the same month, the biggest in British history, raised income tax by 40% to 2s 11½d. By May 1916 the daily cost of the war was £4,820,000. Two months later it was calculated that it was £6 million and by July 1917 it had risen to £7 million.

Despite rises in income tax, this accounted for only around 28% of government revenue, largely because there was a comparatively small number of income tax payers (only 1.13 million at the start of the war, although this had increased to 2.4 million by 1918). This was because income tax did not come into effect until a salary of £160 had been reached. In 1913 the annual income of a salaried middle class worker was £340 and he would be paying 1s 2d in tax – in the April 1918 Budget, this was increased to 6 shillings. In addition, the tax threshold had been lowered to £130, so the middle classes were particularly hard hit.

A series of War Loans was launched to help finance the war, the first being for £350 million. War Savings Certificates were attractive to the small saver as been can be seen by this letter to the Friern Barnet War Savings Association on 10 February 1917:

> "We are much obliged for the figures with which you have been good enough to supply us concerning the sale of War Savings Certificates in Friern Barnet. We understand that with a population of about 15,000, you have sold over 15,000 certificates. This is a most excellent record, and we very heartily congratulate all those who have helped to bring about this most satisfactory result, which is one of which you may one and all be proud."

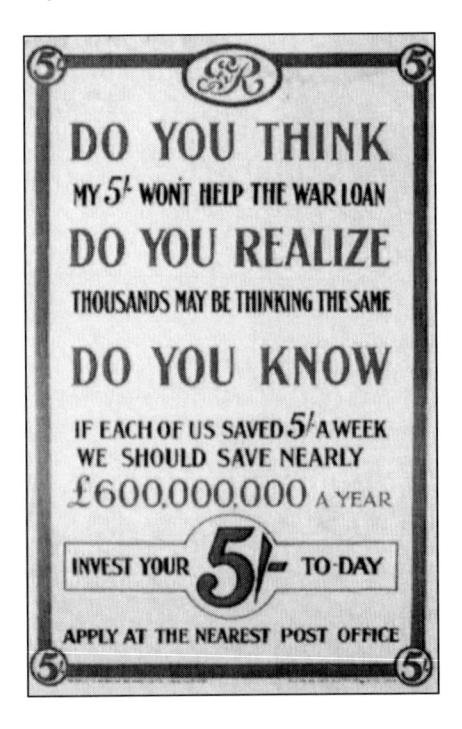

Five bob is all it takes…… (©IWM Art.IWM PST 10280)

Also in Friern Barnet, The All Saints' and St James Association reported on 24 February 1917 that it had been in working order for 22 weeks and in that time 440 War Savings Certificates had been bought and a sum of £340 had been lent to the nation. They urged the scholars at the schools to do their utmost to obtain at least one new member, to obtain at least one purchaser and to increase their own subscriptions. During "War Savings Week" in February takings amounted to £128 15s, a sum ten times greater than the weekly average.

In 1917 the Government introduced War Bonds with 5% interest repayable in 1947 or 4% repayable in 1942, and these were well received; in March 1918 War Bond Week raised over £138 million. There were special events designed to attract savings - a "Tank Week" took place in March 1918 in Trafalgar Square at which a tank was displayed and in October 1918 a replica ruined French village, also in Trafalgar Square for a "Feed the Guns" campaign raised £29 million in just eight days.

J. C. & J. FIELD, Ltd.,

Toilet Soap Experts, Candle Lighting, Wick, and Night Light Manufacturers—one of the very Oldest Firms in the country, established in the reign of Charles I.—have decided to devote this space, usually occupied for advertising their "SIANARA TOILET SOAP," to-day to urge their Customers and Friends to buy

NATIONAL WAR BONDS.

The Security is absolute, and the Yield of Interest makes the purchase of these NATIONAL WAR BONDS an

INVESTMENT OF THE MOST DESIRABLE KIND.

They can be purchased from £5 upwards at any Post Office.

The purchase of these WAR BONDS fulfils

TWO IMPORTANT DUTIES—

1. To assist your Country.
2. To put yourself in a Secure Position, no matter how critical the times may be that are to come.

FACTS about NATIONAL WAR BONDS

THE price of the Bonds is £100 per cent. There are four different series from which to choose those best suited to your requirements—three of them are repayable with a redemption premium.

£5 per cent. Bonds, repayable 1st October, 1922, at 102 per cent.
£5 per cent. Bonds, repayable 1st October, 1924, at 103 per cent.
£5 per cent. Bonds, repayable 1st October, 1927, at 105 per cent.

and

£4 per cent. Bonds, repayable 1st October, 1927, at 100 per cent.
("Income Tax compounded.")

Interest is payable on the 1st April and 1st October. The first dividend payable 1st April, 1918 will be calculated from date of application. Bonds will be issued in denominations of £50, £100, £200, £500, 1,000, and 5,000. Bonds can be to bearer or registered at the Bank of England or Ireland at your option —if registered they can be transferable by deed or transferable in the Bank transfer books as you may desire. If Bonds are registered dividends will be paid to you without deduction of income tax; but if you are liable to income tax you must include such dividends in your own return of income.

Bonds of this issue will be accepted (subject to certain provisions) by the Commissioners of Inland Revenue in satisfaction of amounts due on account of Death Duties, Excess Profits or Munitions Exchequer payments. The Bonds carry the right of conversion into any future loans (except those issued abroad and short-dated securities) which may be issued by the Government for the purpose of carrying on the War. You will find full details, including conversion and other rights, in the official prospectus, copies of which can be obtained at any Bank or Money Order Office—go at once and get a copy and study carefully the terms offered, or—

Ask your Banker or Stockbroker, or apply for 5 per cent. Bonds, Post Office issue, for £5, £10, & £20, at any Bank or Post Office.

Your Local War Savings Committee will advise you in every way.

But invest in National War Bonds to-day

ISSUED BY
THE NATIONAL WAR SAVINGS COMMITTEE,
(Appointed by His Majesty's Treasury).
SALISBURY SQUARE, LONDON, E.C.4.

Finchley War Savings Week.

MONDAY, DECEMBER 4th,
TO
SATURDAY, the 9th, 1916.

DURING this week every Man, Woman, and Child in the District should do something definite in the way of LENDING THEIR MONEY TO THEIR COUNTRY, either by Joining a WAR SAVINGS ASSOCIATION or by investing in 15s. 6d. WAR SAVINGS CERTIFICATES at any Post Office or any Bank.

By Saturday, the 9th of December, everyone should be able to show some definite proof of what he or she has lent to help to win the War.

What will YOU have to show?

Full particulars can be obtained from the Chairman of the Finchley War Savings Committee, C. S. SYRETT, J.P. (Chairman Finchley District Council), 9, The Hawthorns, Finchley; or the Secretary, J. O. HERDMAN "Bathlin," Woodside Grange - road, North Finchley.

Join a War Savings Association,
OR
Buy 15s. 6d. War Savings Certificates.

War bonds not only offered investors a good return on their money, they also gave them a sense of patriotism (Barnet Press)

Further issues of War Bonds were equally successful. In June 1915 £910 million was raised, in May 1916 £300 million, February 1917 £700 million and June 1918 £500 million.

By 1917 the war was accounting for 70% of all Government spending. Despite the other methods of raising money, the most successful proved to be the imposition on industry of a duty on excess profits which was bringing in some 36% of total Government revenue by 1918. Loans from abroad, particularly the United States, made up the rest of the Government's income. From 1914 to 1918 government expenditure as a percentage of gross national product rose from 13.5 to 59.3.

When all the sums were added up after the war, it was revealed that Britain had made loans to the Allies amounting to £1.5 billion, not all of which was repaid.

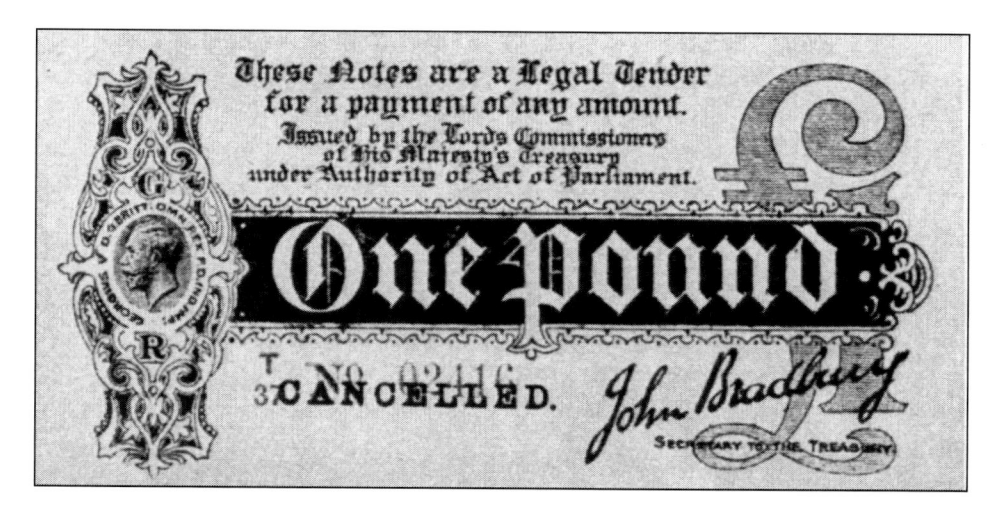

The Government issued new paper money to replace gold sovereigns. Ten shilling notes were red and £1 notes were brown

CHAPTER 8

FEEDING THE FAMILY

At the start of the war Britain was importing some sixty percent of her food. Bacon came from Denmark, butter from Russia, wheat from America and Canada and sugar beet from Germany and Austria. With the increase in demand caused by having to feed the armed forces as well as civilians and the reduction in supply caused by import restrictions it was inevitable that there would be increases in prices which placed heavy burdens on British housewives. Higher prices actually acted as a way of rationing scarce resources but there were never wholesale shortages as in Germany where practically everything was rationed and things like cocoa and fruit were virtually unobtainable.

The average household began to feel the effects of a whole series of price rises although with one less mouth to feed (their husbands or sons being away in France) family budgets could just about cope.

After a year of war meat prices had nearly doubled (neck of mutton had gone up from 2½d to 3d a pound in 1914 to 4½d to 6d by 1915) and the price of wheat had increased by 72% and barley by 40%.

By March 1916 food prices had risen by 48% and in 1916 a poor harvest led to the doubling of the price of potatoes. In the same period flour went up by 66%, bread by 58%, cheese by 52% and bacon by 49%. Even tea, the answer to all an Englishman's problems, went up by 50% and consumers were urged to drink coffee for breakfast as an alternative.

The Board of Trade set up a Food Department under Sir William Beveridge whose job was to handle the distribution of both home produced and imported food. This caused some consternation among the various established suppliers – producers, importers, wholesalers and retailers. The

Household Economy in WAR time!

AT so small a cost as BIRD'S Custard, there are few dishes in our daily diet which provide so much real nourishment and body-building material.

BIRD'S Custard is not only a delectable dainty, enjoyed by everybody, but is also a genuine wholesome food, which may be consumed freely by the children and grown-ups, with the confidence that, money for money, no better value is obtainable.

There is no shortage of BIRD'S Custard. There is plenty for everyone. We are working hard to supply the exceptional demands of the Military and the Public.

Bird's
the Nutritious Custard

IS STILL SOLD AT THE USUAL PRICES.

In Pkts. 2 for 1½d.   Boxes 4d & 7½d.   LARGE 8½d Tins.

This advertisement appeared in the 'Barnet Press' on 8 August 1914, just four days after war was declared!

Government requisitioned food and then set the maximum prices at which it could be sold; this was to try and prevent profiteering. Cheese was one of the first things to be regulated (by an unlikely sounding Cheese Committee) which led to the following comment:

"Government cheese! Government cheese!
Warranted wholesome and flavoured to please;
Food for the nation, a delicate treat,
Fresh from the dairies of Downing Street;
The genuine article needless to mench
Stamped with the seal of the Treasury Bench."

One of the problems was ensuring a sufficient supply of butter and this was replaced by margarine which in itself became scarce and was one of the things that housewives became used to queuing for, along with meat, sugar and bread. In the April 1916 Budget the Government introduced taxes on, amongst other things, mineral waters and there was an increase in taxes on sugar, cocoa and coffee and on motor cars. Sugar in particular was in short supply, because the Government banned the importation of sugar beet in October 1914. As a result between July 1914 and September 1916 the price of sugar rose by 166% and it was eventually rationed in 1918.

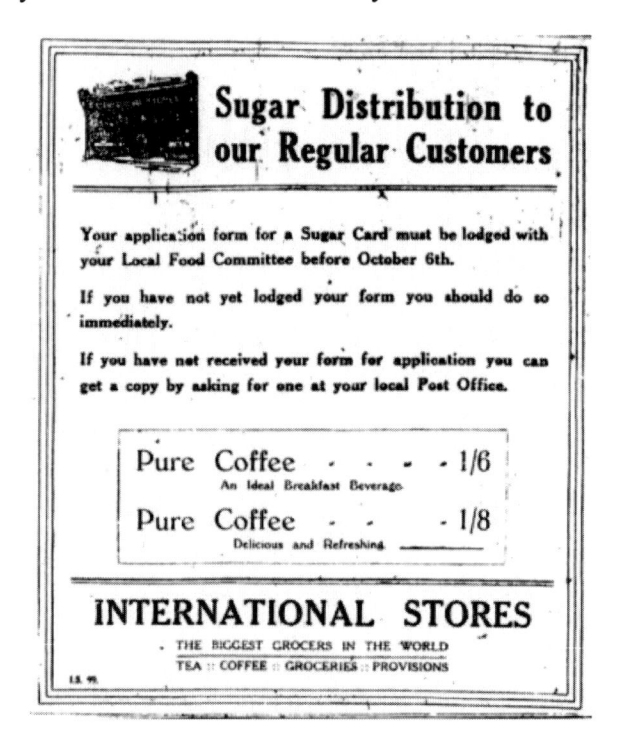

Sugar Distribution to our Regular Customers

Your application form for a Sugar Card must be lodged with your Local Food Committee before October 6th.

If you have not yet lodged your form you should do so immediately.

If you have not received your form for application you can get a copy by asking for one at your local Post Office.

Pure Coffee - - - - 1/6
An Ideal Breakfast Beverage

Pure Coffee - - - - 1/8
Delicious and Refreshing

INTERNATIONAL STORES
THE BIGGEST GROCERS IN THE WORLD
TEA :: COFFEE :: GROCERIES :: PROVISIONS

('Barnet Press' 20 October 1917)

BARNET URBAN FOOD CONTROL COMMITTEE.
HOW TO OBTAIN SUGAR.

IT IS IMPORTANT TO REMEMBER—

(1) That after December 30th you can only obtain Sugar by one of the following systems.

(2) That you can only use the system which applies to your particular case.

A.—THE HOUSEHOLD SYSTEM.

If you have already deposited with your grocer a Household Sugar Card, and If you are still a Member of the same Household :—

You must go to your grocer after December 8th and ask for Declaration Forms. When you have filled these up your grocer will give you a Retailer's Sugar Ticket for each member of the household, which must be shown when buying sugar after December 30th.

B.—THE COUPON SYSTEM.

If you have not registered with your grocer on a Household Sugar Card, or If you have left the household from which you were registered you must go to a Post Office before December 15th, ask for an application form, fill it up and post it as directed. You will later receive a Ration Paper which will entitle you to get Sugar Coupons from a Post Office.

H. W POOLE, Executive Officer,
W. PLUMPTON, A. E DOLTON, Deputy Executive Officers.

Municipal Offices, Wood Street, Barnet, 5th December, 1917.

('Barnet Press' 8 December 1917)

The shortage of sugar affected not just housewives but also producers of beer, confectionery and chocolate, whilst jam making virtually ceased. Alternatives such as syrup, glucose and honey were pressed into service and restaurants ceased the practice of leaving bowls of sugar on tables for their customers to help themselves.

In retaliation for the Royal Navy blockading German ports, in 1916 Germany increased the use of submarines (U-boats) in the Atlantic which resulted in the loss of some 300,000 tons of Allied merchant shipping. On 1 February 1917 Germany declared that it would now conduct unrestricted submarine warfare; the result was that 1197 merchant ships were lost and the effect on the import of food was dramatic.

To counteract the threat of severe shortages the Government introduced several measures. A Public Meals Order was introduced on 5 December 1916 which limited meals in restaurants during the day to two courses and evening meals to three courses. In April 1917 a further Public Meals Order was issued which restricted the amount of food that hotels, restaurants and boarding houses could serve. On Tuesdays in London no meat, poultry or game could be served and potatoes could only be served on that day. The amount of meat was rationed to 5 ounces at lunch and 5 ounces at dinner; bread was restricted to 2 ounces at each meal. To ensure that the rules were being obeyed, managers had to keep registers of invoices and other paperwork relating to the purchase and serving of food. Yet another Public Meals Order in February 1918 established quite specific restrictions. There were to be two meatless meals a week (Tuesday and Friday in London) and no milk was to be consumed as a beverage, except with tea, coffee or cocoa. Guests had to provide their own sugar and not more than 1½ ounces of bread, cakes, buns, scones or biscuits could be served with afternoon teas. Breakfast in hotels was a difficult meal to cater for as milk was not allowed on porridge and bacon was forbidden, so a typical breakfast would consist of fish, eggs, jam, and bread and butter. A fairly substantial dinner could be served without contravening regulations - hors d'oeuvres, soup, fish, a meatless entrée, a portion of poultry or game, pudding and a dessert. Meat had to be weighed uncooked and with bone and poultry and game could include rabbits, hares, and "any kind of bird killed for food." There was one exception to the Order; public eating places who did not charge more than 1s 2d for a meal, exclusive of beverages, were exempt, as were those who charged less than 5d for meals (again excluding beverages) which were served between 3pm and 5.30pm. This was to help working men to get cheap meals.

On 3 February 1917 a scheme of Voluntary Rationing was introduced and consumers were urged to limit their consumption, however this was not well received and it was later dropped.

(©IWM Art.IWM PST 6569)

In November 1917 tests had been carried out by the Ministry of Food in conjunction with the Food Production Department which showed that the use of potatoes in bread rendered the bread much more palatable and of better texture than that made from just flour alone and it also kept longer. A recipe was issued for those having the time to bake bread at home:

"7lb of flour

1½oz. salt

2oz Yeast

3½lb. Water

½lb. Potatoes

The potatoes should be washed and boiled in their skins. When ready they should be strained, peeled and mashed. Then weigh ½lb of potatoes to 7lb. of flour. Put the flour, salt and potatoes into a basin and mix well. Heat up to 82 degrees. Dissolve the yeast in the 3½lb. of water, which should be maintained at a temperature of 90 degrees. Then add the yeast mixture to the flour, salt and potatoes. Mix the whole well and knead for ten minutes. Place on a table free from draughts for 1½ hours, then knead again and cover up for one hour more. The mixture may then be divided into pieces of equal size, moulded into the shape required and placed in slightly warmed and greased tins. Allow it to rise for thirty minutes before placing it in the oven. Bake at a temperature of 420 degrees. Loaves of 1lb. weight will bake in half an hour. Two-pound loaves will take fifty minutes to bake. As experience is gained it will be found that the quantity of potatoes can be increased form ½lb. to 1lb."

The growing lack of bread meant that rationing was an increasing possibility. The *Barnet Press* of 12 May 1917 stated:

"The decision as to bread tickets does not yet appear to have been reached. While many are of the opinion that, should the absence of food stocks demand it, compulsory economy should be imposed at once there are others who still earnestly hope that the good sense and self-control of the great body of English people will do away with the necessity for bread tickets altogether."

A poster from 1917 (©IWM Art.IWM PST6541)

The *Barnet Press* continued to publicise the problems with food and on 12 May 1917 it reported:

> "Food appears to be plentiful though dear. Why not buy it? To enlighten and help these people, committees are at work in our district organising meetings and demonstrations. At the public meeting in Friary Park on Saturday May 19th at 5pm well-known public speakers will place the facts of the food position plainly before us. Mrs Hudson Lyall, one of the great authorities on this matter, has already addressed upward of five hundred gatherings. Miss Manley, of the Board of Education, has promised to open the great food demonstration week at Holly Park Council School on Saturday, May 26th at 3pm. This proposed food demonstration has already attracted wide interest and support. Its helpfulness will go straight to the heart and mind of every thrifty housewife. It is comparatively simple for a food committee to advise the public to "eat less bread." It is much more difficult to indicate successfully how to do with less bread. It is just this problem which the Friern Barnet Committee have tackled so vigorously. Visitors to the food demonstration will not only be shown just what to buy instead of bread, but, more important still, how to prepare and cook the bread substitute so as to ensure the maintenance of health."

An editorial in *Barnet Press* on 26 May 1917 gave some advice to housewives:

> "The stress on our food supplies set up by the war will not be wholly a bad thing if it teaches us to be more economical – less wasteful – than in the easy years which have gone. We know that in Holland, Denmark and France (to go no further from home) the cuisine makes appetising and sustaining food of things which we have been in the habit of wasting. How few British housewives know that peapods are a first-rate base for soup, and that even the water vegetables have been cooked in has a food value. Waste is waste, whether we live in times of prosperity or in time of stress,

and perhaps it is well that, from time to time, the crime of waste should be made plain to us."

A piece in the *Barnet Press* of 7 July 1917 recommended salmon as a cheap food:

> "Choice canned salmon has proved a blessing to the housewife in the present days of high food prices, and the clever cook can use it in so many different ways that the family will never tire of it. The following salmon dishes are particularly successful: Salmon Rissoles, Salmon Kedgeree, Scalloped Salmon, Salmon Timbales, Salmon Rolls, Salmon Puree or Salmon Paste. Messrs Harvey and Shillingford of 11 King's Parade, Church End, Finchley, will be pleased to give recipes for these and other salmon dishes upon request. They report that they still have a good stock of salmon at moderate prices, the half pound tins ranging from 7½d to 11½d each and the one pound tins from 11½d to 1s 6½d, and every tin bears their well-known guarantee 'Money returned in full unless absolutely satisfactory.'"

In December 1917 a Food Vigilance Committee was formed at a meeting in the Congregational Church Hall in Friern Barnet Road and a resolution was passed:

> "That owing to the very acute shortage now being experienced, affecting a considerable number of essential items such as food, we submit that the time has arrived when the Government must undertake the task of rationing all foodstuffs; and, we further submit that the necessary proportion of commodities rationed shall be definitely allocated to the People's Association, namely the Co-operative Societies, in order that these societies may be in a position to distribute the proper quota to each household represented by the membership."

The acute shortage referred to had arisen because of panic buying across the country, although there was no actual shortage of most food and the 1917 harvest had been a record one. The Government was therefore forced to introduce rationing for meat, butter and margarine with effect from 25 February 1918 in London and the Home Counties and then throughout the whole country. Ration cards were issued and consumers were urged to register with their local retailer, although the card could be used anywhere. Helpful lectures were introduced which gave consumers ideas for making the best of limited supplies.

Ena Constable, who was fifteen at the time, described the conditions in Whetstone to Barnet local historian Gillian Gear:

> "I can remember queuing at the shops and not knowing what I was queuing for. There was a grocers shop opposite our premises and if we saw one or two people gathered there we would join in and not know what it was, whether fats or cheese or whatever. I lined up once and found it was cheese and found that the man had cut it up into portions of 2d per portion. An old wanderer was ahead of me and went in and said "Pennorth please, guv'nor" and the man said "2 pennorth" and the man said "Have you got a knife?" and the shopkeeper said "Yes" and the man took the knife and cut it in half and said "That's a pennorth", put down his penny and left the other half there. I suppose that was all he had to spend."

Ena recalled that every Saturday night her father would go over to the butchers on the corner by the *Bull and Butcher* pub in Whetstone to get something for Sunday dinner. He would not know what he was going to get; it depended on what was left, but the butcher always saved them something.

On 6 April 1917 a Food Hoarding Order prohibited anyone from buying more than the family actually needed and powers were given to search

FINCHLEY URBAN DISTRICT COUNCIL.

By arrangement with the Middlesex Education Committee,

PUBLIC DEMONSTRATIONS in WAR-TIME COOKERY

Will be given at the Council's DOMESTIC SUBJECTS CENTRES as under:—

DAILY at 3 and 7 p.m.

During the Week commencing MONDAY, JUNE 18th, at
104, HIGH STREET, NORTH FINCHLEY.

During the Week commencing MONDAY, JUNE 25th, at
The Cookery Centre, NORTH ROAD COUNCIL SCHOOL, EAST FINCHLEY.

Residents are invited to confer with the Cookery Teachers, who will be in attendance daily from 2 p.m., upon matters relative to Food Economy and Food Substitutes.

PLEASE BRING NOTEBOOK AND PENCIL.

MINISTRY OF FOOD.

Important Notice.

MR. KENNEDY JONES, M.P.,
DIRECTOR-GENERAL OF FOOD ECONOMY,

will Address a Public Meeting at the
LECTURE HALL, HIGH ROAD, East Finchley,

On the real facts concerning

FOOD SUPPLY

And the bearing thereon of the

WAR SITUATION,

on

Saturday Evening, April 14th.

At 8 o'clock.

Chair will be taken by
C. S. SYRETT, Esq.,
Chairman of the Finchley Urban District Council.

Advertisements in 'Barnet Press'

people's homes. On 18 April 1917 pastry and cake making were restricted. An example of the serious bread situation was shown on 2 June 1917 when George Brannan of Lonsdale Cottages, High Road, East Finchley was fined at Highgate Petty Sessions £50 or two months' imprisonment for having used bread made of wheaten flour to be fed to his pigs at Barton's Farm, Summers Lane. In his defence Brannan, who had 51 pigs, said that the bread was old and unfit for human consumption and that he thought he was doing his duty to the country by turning the old bread into pork. The following week a letter in *Barnet Press* from a baker defended Mr Brannan:

> "I am a baker of 50 years standing and am puzzled to know what we bakers are to do with our stale bread, for it is quite impossible to know exactly what quantity of bread our customers require daily. We can not sell it, for nobody will have stale bread and if we give it to horses and pigs we are liable to a very heavy fine. Perhaps one of your numerous readers may be able to suggest a way for us out of our difficulty."

The 8 October 1917 issue of *The Observer* reported that Edmonton Council had sold over fifty tons of seed potatoes. These would have been bought by people who were growing their own food as one thing that did help to reduce food shortages was the introduction of allotments in 1917 under the Land Cultivation Order. It was made clear that this would only be in place for the duration of the war and allotment holders were therefore advised not to spend money on fencing them in. In fact, allotments were to become so valuable that anyone caught stealing from them was fined £100. At a meeting at Holly Park School in Friern Barnet on 18 January 1917 it was stated that there had been 466 applicants for 36 acres of allotments; by April the number of applicants had increased to 734.

To create an allotment it was first necessary to break up the soil and the Board of Agriculture, the Royal Horticultural Society and the Vacant Land Cultivation Society urged that this be done as a matter of some urgency. There was reticence by some members to working on Sundays but it was argued that if soldiers could fight on Sundays and special constables could be on duty on Sundays it would not be very wrong for civilians to cultivate on Sundays (*cries of "Hear, hear" from the audience*). The *Barnet Press* started publishing a weekly column "Hints for Allotment Holders" which gave useful tips for novices.

Mabel Holman was one of those who joined the allotment movement, although her initial thoughts were against the idea, as her letter of 24 January 1917 shows:

> "Everyone is getting allotments at Muswell Hill – you can get 140 feet for 1/- a year on which to grow vegetables. Three of our neighbours have some in the fields at the end of our road and are anxious for us to do the same, but I'm afraid it would be too hard work for us – fancy digging up fields (170 feet x 80 feet) but it is a splendid chance for anyone who has a man in the house – all parts are doing it now – even dear old Richmond Park is being cut up to grow potatoes – sacrilege is it not?"

The offer of help changed her mind and she and her sister obviously enjoyed the experience, and the free food:

> "We are going "plotting". We have joined a noble band of cabbage patchers. Mr Beecher has persuaded us to have a quarter of his and has very kindly offered to get the hard digging done for us. So now we are deeply involved in the relative virtues of spuds, "early, middle and lates" and up to our eyes in seed catalogues. We have not seen our actual piece of land yet, but it is the fields down Coppetts Lane." (*13 April 1917*)

> "Our plot is full up now. Beets and parsnips already coming up. Win and I spent nearly the whole weekend on it and in the words of Win: "Returned to office on Monday for a rest." There are two old countrymen down there and they are helping us and we get all sorts of hints from them and also new-laid eggs from their home – a

cottage down Coppetts Lane. I go down nearly every night for an hour and watch the spuds sprouting." *(9 May 1917)*

"Our plot is doing well – we have had loads of peas and I have already picked nearly 30lbs. Also beets and beans, in fact, it has been quite a success and the peas are lovely (marrowfats) and the envy of other plotters. We have people come to see them. It is the only place I can feel at all happy, out in the fresh air and fields." *(25 July 19717)*

(©Image; IWM Art. IWM PST 10826)

At St James' School in Friern Barnet Lane the boys had placed at their disposal a large piece of land for the purpose of growing vegetables. The land consisted of 12 large plots, each in charge of two boys, and potatoes had been planted. The boys were described as "being very enthusiastic, and as, in their aprons and with a spade on shoulder, they march to their "war gardens" they look extremely fit and workmanlike."

(©Image; IWM Art.IWM PST 5233)

East Barnet Valley Urban District Council.

PIG-KEEPING.

PURSUANT to the power vested in them by Regulation 2.O. of the Order in Council of the 10th January, 1917, the above Council grants permission generally to the Residents within their area to KEEP PIGS, notwithstanding or contrary to any provisions of any Byelaw made by them which is for the time being in force prohibiting, restricting, or regulating the keeping of Pigs, subject, however, to the observance of any directions which may be given by the Council in the interests of public health.

T. A. BUCKLEY,
Clerk to the Council.

Council Offices,
New Barnet.
22nd February, 1917.

('Barnet Press' 24 Feb 1917)

BARNET URBAN DISTRICT COUNCIL.
Food Economy Committee.

WASTE NOT. WANT NOT.

THE COMMITTEE MAKE THIS MOST URGENT APPEAL TO THE PEOPLE OF BARNET :—

TO SAVE COAL. Use as little as possible, and Burn all Cinders.

TO SAVE WASTE PAPER, BOTTLES, TINS of every description, CLOTH CUTTINGS, etc., etc., and bring them to the Central Depot (which will be announced later), or communicate with the Secretary at address given below if Collection is desired.

CARRY HOME YOUR OWN PARCELS.

Remember, that for every Ton of so-called "Waste" collected a Ton of Transport is released for use by the Government.

Please address all communications to—

F. E. JENNINGS,
Barnet Food Economy Committee,
Municipal Offices,
Wood-street,
Barnet.

('Barnet Press' 8 Dec 1917)

An idea of the importance of food production, particularly of wheat for bread, can be seen from this advertisement in *Barnet Press* of 10 March 1917:

FARM LABOUR.

SOLDIERS FOR FARM WORK.

Farmers wishing to secure Soldier Labour for spring cultivation should apply to the

CLERK OF THE HERTFORDSHIRE WAR AGRICULTURAL COMMITTEE 28 CASTLE STREET HERTFORD

without delay.

Soldiers will be sent FREE to the nearest Railway Station. Farmers must pay current Rate of Wages for the District as fixed by the Committee.

INTERNED CIVILIAN PRISONERS.

Farmers wishing to obtain the labour of Interned Civilian Prisoners should also apply for particulars and form of application to same address.

CHARLES E. LONGMORE, Clerk.

28, Castle-street, Hertford,
7th March, 1917.

Standing in a queue for hours - an everyday occurrence in 1918

Hay boxes were used for completing the cooking of partially cooked foods

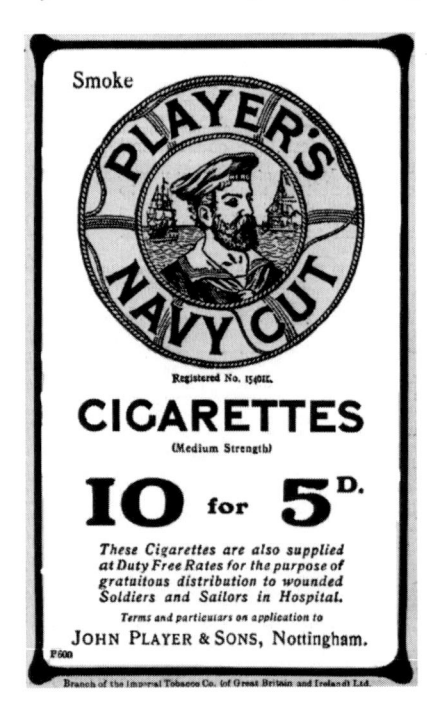

Advertisements from 1917 with a wartime theme

Food manufacturers found new uses for their products or created new ones

No eggs…….

EVERY RAID HAS A SILVER LINING
THANKFUL SHOPPER: "Ah, well, it's a mercy it wasn't to-morrer!"

…….and no sugar

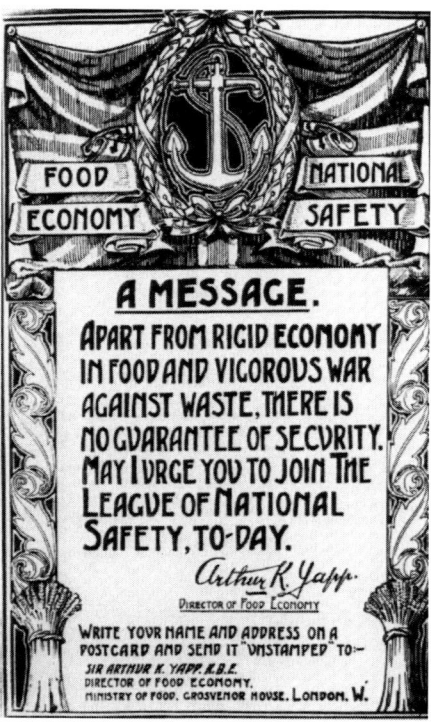

Advertisements in "My Magzine" April 1916

It was a tribute to some of the sensible Government measures made under DORA and the contributions made by allotment holders (there were some 800,000 allotments by the end of the war) and women agricultural workers that nobody starved in Britain. There may have been shortages of certain items and rationing, queuing and increased prices had become a part of everyday life but the British public accepted that restrictions were necessary and ensured fairness for all.

CHAPTER 9

RESTRICTIONS AT HOME

Life at home was made harder by some unforeseen events. The War Office and the Admiralty requisitioned 1319 London buses (about 41% of the total) which were sent to France, along with their crews, to be used as troop transport. This, combined with petrol rationing and shortage of staff, meant greatly reduced bus services with some routes being withdrawn altogether. As if this was not bad enough, fares went up by a third between 1916 and 1918.

One account of bus travel shows how bad conditions were, despite a relaxation in police regulations which allowed standing passengers in buses for the first time:

This 'B type' bus had been converted by the Army into a travelling loft for carrier pigeons

"Getting home during rush hours was a daily terror, especially on dark winter evenings in London. The crowds of office workers were vastly increased and the scramble to get into some of the longer distance trams and omnibuses constituted a bear fight out of which those of both sexes, who were worsted or driven off the overladen vehicles by the conductors, retreated to the pavements with hat bashed in, umbrellas broken, shins and ankles kicked and bruised, in a dazed and shaken condition."

Throughout the war restrictions on things other than food were being imposed thick and fast. In October 1915 licensed premises were forced to close at 10pm instead of 11pm and in November there were restrictions on the opening hours of clubs.

One innovation was the introduction in May 1916 of British Summer Time which by giving lighter evenings was of particular help to farmers. It has, of course, been with us ever since.

In the April 1916 Budget the Government imposed a tax on the price of cinema tickets, 1d on those costing up to 6d and 2d on those between 6d and 1s 2d. Like many increases in prices this did not affect the better-off but was an added burden to the working classes. In September 1916 the *Barnet Press* reported that Barnet Fair was a shadow of its former self despite the presence of a large number of men of military age: "it seems absurd to think that so many healthy men should be physically unfit" was their comment. The *Daily Chronicle* said "within a few miles there was a much greater attraction; the wrecked Zeppelin."

Many entertainment and sporting events were suspended during the war including league football and the Boat Race and centres of culture such as the British Museum and the Tate Gallery closed for the duration. However, people needed a release and dance halls, cinemas, music halls and theatres did a roaring trade. The *Barnet Press* carried this advertisement on 24 June 1916:

Lord JOHN SANGER'S
(ALL BRITISH INSTITUTION)
Royal Circus & Menagerie
(The Original and Only Sanger's Circus).

UNDERHILL, BARNET,
Friday, June 30th.

IMPORTANT & EXCLUSIVE ENGAGEMENT OF

The Great Russian Cossack Troupe.

A Brilliant and Fearless Exhibition of Riding, National Peasant Dances, and Manœuvres, terminating by a Realistic Exhibition of how these wonderful sons of Russia face, fight, and defeat their enemies in War. Whilst galloping at full speed they will leap from one horse to another, and to escape detection throw themselves from the saddle, hanging in the stirrup by one foot with the body dragging at full length upon the ground. These wonderful riders are not circus performers, but are the pick of Russia's finest horsemen, who are unfortunately debarred from taking their part in the great European conflict.

PIMPO'S GREATEST ABSURDITY.
The TWO WILLIES, introducing THE TURK to THE BRITISH LION, in which PIMPO exhibits his Ship of the Desert. Sixty Laughs a Minute.

THE BEAUTIFUL DELLA CASSA SISTERS.
THREE LADIES. THREE ELEPHANTS. THREE HORSES. A Most Wonderful Exhibition.

SANGER'S PURE WHITE TWIN HORSES,
Introduced by FRANCESCA, in an Exhibition of High School Riding and Driving.

PIMPO, the Great & Inimitable, will display his varied accomplishments at each performance.

THE WONDERFUL PERFORMING SEA LIONS,
The Greatest Animal Act in the World.

For this Town only.
THE AERIAL DANES, in a most Thrilling Performance.

And other Items in a Long and Varied Programme too numerous to mention.

TWO PERFORMANCES--at 3 and 8 p.m.
POPULAR PRICES OF ADMISSION.

In Friern Barnet the North Middlesex Golf Club suffered from a drop in membership due to younger members being called up and older ones having little time for leisure activities. The few German and Austrian members were asked not to use the club's facilities during the war. Half of the course was turned over to the growing of hay which members harvested. Areas were also given over to growing vegetables. Returning wounded soldiers and those on leave were welcome to play. At the nearby Friary Park Bowling Club there was also a big reduction in membership and few matches were played; in 1918 the fixture list was suspended altogether.

Wounded soldiers on the eighteenth green at North Middlesex Golf Club

In Central London the more expensive restaurants were doing good business. Maison Lyons had four large public rooms and even had a Dixieland band. The waitresses, forerunners to the famous "Nippys", wore a distinctive uniform of black and white cap, a front buttoned black dress with white collar and cuffs, white apron, black stockings and black low-heeled shoes. A pad and pencil was attached to their belt.

Maison Lyons

"In Oxford St., opposite Bond St. Tube Station."

OPENS MONDAY SEPTEMBER 11th

To mark the opening of their latest establishment the Directors of J. Lyons & Co., Ltd., are devoting **HALF THE TOTAL RECEIPTS ON THE OPENING DAY TO THE "STAR AND GARTER FUND,"** which is to furnish and equip a home for permanently disabled sailors and soldiers, to occupy the famous site on Richmond Hill.

The following ladies and gentlemen interested in this fund have kindly promised to assist in the Confectionery Salon and Restaurant on the opening day:—

Winifred Countess of Arran
The Countess of Derby
The Lady Cowdray
Lady Booth
Lady Raphael
The Hon. Mrs. Henry McLaren
Mrs. Louis Duveen
Mrs. Colefax
Mrs. Gerald du Maurier
Mrs. Dennis Eadie
Miss Lilian Braithwaite
Miss Doris Keane
Miss May Whitty
Miss Violet Loraine
Mlle. Nielka
Miss Ruby Miller
Miss Lydia Bilbenke
Miss Laura Cowie
Miss Gladys Cooper
Miss Rosalie Toller
Miss Phyllis Broughton
Miss Unity More
Miss Marie Hemingway
Miss Hilda Bavley
Miss Dorothy Faine
Miss Stella St. Audrie
Miss Nina Boucicault
Miss Sybil Duncombe
Mrs. G. P. Huntley
Miss Dorothy King
Miss Mary Glynne
Miss Amy Ravenscroft
Mrs. Crossy
Mr. Arthur Wontner
Mr. Maison Keys
Mr. Edward Knoblauch
Mr. Marsh Allen
Mr. Malcolm Cherry
Mr. Ben Webster

THE new Maison Lyons, situated in the very heart of shopland, incorporates the largest and most beautifully appointed salon in Europe devoted to the sale of *Confiserie & Patisserie*. Here, in infinite variety, may be found Dainty Confections prepared by the most accomplished and highly trained chefs from the finest ingredients that a thorough knowledge of the world's markets can provide.

This new Maison Lyons is also a super-café of character, providing entertainment in keeping with the call for war-time economy.
"CORNER HOUSE" PRICES.

The Restaurant section, which is open daily until 11 p.m., and fully licensed, of the new Maison Lyons is capable of accommodating over 1,000 persons, and provides recherché yet inexpensive fare amidst surroundings of artistic distinction and charm. "Corner House" Tariff and Prices. Vocal and Orchestral Music all day. In the Confectionery Salon is the most up-to-date Soda Fountain for supplying Iced Fruit and other special American drinks.

J. LYONS & Co., Ld., *Proprietors*

A wonderful display of Table Dainties may be seen at the Maison Lyons Salons.
THE CHOCOLATERIE PAR EXCELLENCE OF THE WORLD.
The prices are reasonable, and many varieties, hitherto made exclusively abroad, are now produced at the new Maison Lyons. Experience and a large output combine to give Lyons' Chocolates the premier position as the finest sweetmeats produced. Prices 4/6, 3/6 & 2/6 per lb. Every kind of sweetmeats and bonbons, including American Candies, is freshly made daily on the premises.

PATISSERIE, Etc.

Fours de Soirée	1/9 dozen
Petits Fours Glacés	2/6 lb.
Fondants Fourrés	2/6 lb.
French Pastries	3/- dozen
Entremets de Table	from 1/-
Fancy Gateaux	1/3 - 3/-
Bonbons Variés	from 1/- lb.
Marrons Glacés	4/- lb.

Plain and Fancy Cakes of all kinds.

Concert every evening during dinner.
Mr. **GEORGE CARVEY**
and
THE LADIES' ORCHESTRA
(Under the direction of Miss Margaret Holloway).

THE RAGTIME SEXTET

('Barnet Press' 9 September 1916)

In *Out and About: A Note-Book of London in War-time* Thomas Burke described the change in London in 1917:

> "The Strand… is blocked for pedestrian traffic by Australians and New Zealanders; Piccadilly Circus belongs to the Belgians and the French; and the Americans possess Belgravia. Canadian cafeterias are doing good business round Westminster; French coffee-bars are thriving in the Shaftesbury Avenue district; Belgian restaurants occupy the waste corners around Kingsway; and two more Chinese restaurants lately opened in the West End."

On 5 May 1917 flat racing was suspended for the duration as there was a shortage of oats. Even throwing rice at weddings was made a criminal offence.

1917 saw the addition of further DORA restrictions, some of which might have seemed rather bizarre, including sending abroad any letter written in invisible ink; trespassing on railways or loitering near railway arches, bridges or tunnels; and buying binoculars without official authorisation. Church bells could not be rung and nobody was allowed to light bonfires or fireworks. Perhaps the most draconian of the laws was the one that allowed the Government to take over any factory or workshop or any piece of land. Not unsurprisingly it was forbidden to talk about navy or military matters in public places or to spread rumours about military matters.

The winter of 1917 was particularly cold and coal rationing was introduced in London and people besieged coal merchants armed with baskets, buckets and prams. *The Observer* of 8 April 1917 described the scene:

> "The usual week-end potato and coal scenes took place in London yesterday. At Edmonton 131 vehicles were lined up at the gates of a coal depot at nine o'clock in the morning, while the crowd numbered several hundreds. There were also bread and potato queues of such a length that the police had to regulate them, and newcomers had to inquire which was the particular queue that they wanted."

One of the reasons for the coal shortage was the export of coal to France, most of whose coal mines were in territory occupied by the Germans. Paper, too, was in short supply and waste paper was almost as expensive as new paper. Newspapers were reduced in size and the number of propaganda posters being produced was limited.

With the increased freedom that women had achieved came a loosening of morals and the arrival in London of young women who, often through economic necessity, practised amateur prostitution led in March 1918 to the Government issuing Regulation 40D of DORA to try and protect troops:

> "No woman who is suffering from venereal disease in a communicable form shall have sexual intercourse with any member

of His Majesty's forces or solicit or invite any member of His Majesty's forces to have sexual intercourse with her. If any woman acts in contravention of this regulation she shall be guilty of a summary offence against these regulations. A woman charged with an offence under this regulation shall, if she so requires, be remanded for a period (not less than a week) for the purpose of such medical examination as may be requisite for ascertaining whether she is suffering from such a diseased aforesaid. The defendant shall be informed of her rights to be remanded as aforesaid, and that she may be examined by her own Doctor or by the Medical Officer of the Prison. In this regulation the expression 'venereal disease' means syphilis, gonorrhoea or soft chancre."

The increasing number of casualties returning from the Front was causing problems throughout the country due to the lack of hospital beds. Consequently temporary emergency hospitals were set up in any suitable buildings, from village halls to country houses. In the local area, Avenue House in East End Road, which was used as a hospital for airmen, Grovelands House, Southgate and Ewen Hall in Wood Street, Barnet were pressed into service. These temporary hospitals were staffed by Voluntary Aid Detachments (known popularly as VADs), who were not professional nurses but performed a very useful service in looking after patients and acting as ambulance drivers, cooks, kitchen maids and house maids, clerks and laundresses both at home and at the Front, although not in front line service. The VAD organisation was formed in 1909 as a joint effort by the Red Cross and the Order of St John and grew to 74,000 during the war, two thirds of which were women.

Injured soldiers undergoing treatment in hospitals were issued with distinctive blue suits and red ties so that they could be easily recognised as someone who had served at the Front and therefore worthy of respect.

CHAPTER 10

THE DEMON DRINK

In the early days of the war the *Barnet Press* published lists of Belgian refugees who had arrived in the area. The lists, under the heading "Belgische Vluchtelingen" gave their names, their former address in Belgium and their current address in Barnet and were designed so that they could communicate with each other.

As many as 38,000 Belgian refugees were given temporary shelter and clothing in Alexandra Palace between the outbreak of war and March 1915. Many of these had arrived without any belongings and local appeals were made for contributions of clothing and discarded boots. In December 1914 The Southgate Urban District Council had sent a letter to every house in the district inhabited by guests from Belgium:

> "The Chairman, Vice Chairman, Members and Officers of the Council send hearty greetings to the Belgian guests at ………on the occasion of the New Year, and desire to express a sincere hope that during their sojourn amongst us they may enjoy health and comfort; that 1915 may soon bring victory to the arms of their heroic King and nation and their Allies, and a complete liberation of Belgian soil from the yoke of its villainous invader, compensation for its grievous injuries so nobly borne and a restoration to the peaceful pursuit of the highest attributes of humanity for all time. Long Live Belgium!"

In January 1915 a 'patriotic social evening' was held at the newly built Church Hall of St Michael's, New Southgate at which some Belgian refugees were guests. Women rallied to the cause and in January 1915 the Friern Barnet (North Ward) Ladies Committee reported that they had made close upon two thousand articles, chiefly warm garments and pillows.

Among those benefiting were the British Red Cross Society, the Belgian refugees at Alexandra Palace and wounded soldiers at the Great Northern Hospital.

In 1916 the Palace was used as an internment camp for 1600 German and 700 Austrian troops; some of these were still there in 1919 and the Palace and Park were not opened again to the general public until the end of March 1920.

However, not everyone was putting all their efforts into the war. In particular, it was felt that some workers were giving less than they should and that heavy drinking was playing a part in this. Lloyd George said that they 'were doing more damage than the enemy'. The Government created powers under DORA for local authorities to limit the opening hours in public houses, a 'temporary measure' that, like the 'temporary' income tax that was introduced to fund the Napoleonic War, lasted much longer than intended. In fact, licensing laws were not relaxed until November 2005. After September 1914 pubs were closed after 9.00pm. In November 1915 further controls were introduced under the Liquor Control Regulations, part of DORA. From then on, opening hours were reduced to noon to 2.30pm and 6pm to 9pm and off licences had to close at 8.00pm. Beer was watered down and spirits reduced in strength to not less than 30° under proof. Buying a drink at the bar for someone else, even a relative, was made a criminal offence; 'generous measures' were outlawed as was the practice of running a slate to pay for drinks.

On 5 April 1915 King George V announced that he was prohibiting the use of alcoholic drinks in any of the royal households and there then followed a number of campaigns to 'sign the pledge' and foreswear the use of alcohol. To further deter people from drinking, a tax on drink was introduced on 29 April 1915.

The King's Pledge read: "Following the great example of His Majesty the King, Lord Kitchener and other Ministers of the Crown, I hereby pledge myself to abstain from intoxicating drinks as beverages until the close of the war" was duly signed by many and there were several public meetings like the one at the Lecture Hall, Bellevue Road, Friern Barnet on Monday 5 April 1915 which had been called by the Rector of Friern Barnet, Rev. E Gage Hall and the minister of the Congregational Church, New Southgate, the Rev. E.J. Dukes. In the speeches that were given at the meeting:

> "The object of the meeting was to give people an opportunity of signing the pledge and of setting an example to those weaker brethren whose conduct in this grave crisis was a matter of great concern for the country as a whole *(loud applause)*.......they had been shocked by the statistics produced in regard to the delay and inefficiency in work consequent upon the drinking that prevailed among a section of the workmen. The soldiers had shown great self-sacrifice, and he thought it was the duty of the people at home to show self-sacrifice to whatever extent may be required. By the force of example in abstaining from drink, people would show a good

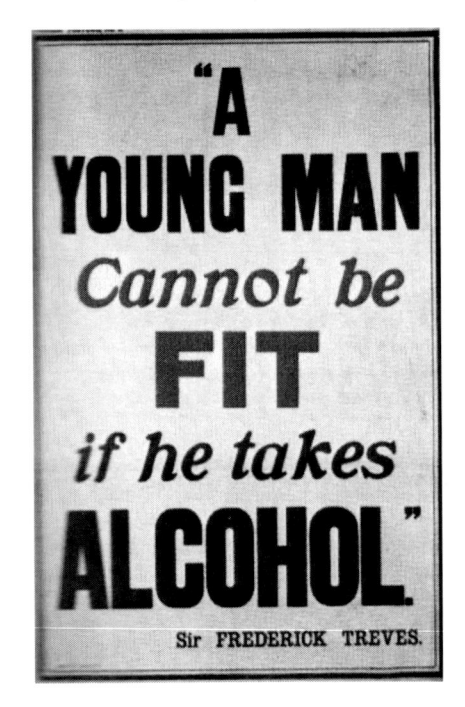

A temperance poster

example that would have far-reaching effects "I ask you solemnly to view the situation fairly and squarely and ask yourself: 'Can I do anything by sacrificing my glass of beer, wine or spirits? Will this help? Of course it will help, and no man can tell what the power of example may be. It is for you to say 'I will play the man and do the best I can for the sake of my country *(loud applause).*"

Apparently of the 115 people who attended the meeting, 99 signed the pledge and those who had signed would be receiving badges. A further 65 people who had attended a meetings at the Congregational Church on Sunday afternoons had also signed the pledge.

In the 5 June issue of *Barnet Press* reported:

"The Rector of Friern Barnet says that in these days of excessive ease and luxury, when personal comfort is so largely considered, the fact that at the public meeting at the Lecture Hall one hundred people took the King's Pledge may be considered, on the whole, satisfactory. The call to associate ourselves, however distantly, with the self-sacrifice of our gallant lads at the Front should appeal to us very strongly, and if we cannot take our stand by them in the fighting line, at least we should not only be willing to "endure" a measure of "hardness as good soldiers" but count it a privilege to be allowed to do so. The non-combatant who can take the pledge and is too selfish to do so, has no earthly right to demand conscription, since he is asking that others may be forced to an act of self-sacrifice in which he refuses, even remotely, to participate."

The growth throughout Europe of socialism led to challenges to Governments and workers were no longer content to accept poor pay and conditions. A continual critic of the war was Keir Hardie, a pacifist and one of the founder members of the Independent Labour Party, forerunner to today's Labour Party. He tried in vain to organise a general strike in protest against the war. Despite an agreement between the Government and the trade unions which guaranteed there would be no strikes, some actually took place including on Clydeside and among coal miners in Wales. Even the Metropolitan Police went on strike for a day in August 1918. Nevertheless in 1916 a meeting of trade union delegates representing nearly two million workers voted by a majority of five to one that Britain should continue the war until Germany was defeated. Other prominent critics of the war included the philosopher Bertrand Russell and Charlotte Despard, a founder member of the Suffragette movement.

A letter from a soldier in Belgium in April 1915 probably summed up the feelings of the men at the Front:

> "I have just read in one of the newspapers that some of the workers at Liverpool have defied Lord Kitchener, and refused to work. What a fine state of things for us to read of. I wonder if they know how proud we feel of them, working out here to keep them safe in their own homes while they are wrangling over a few pence. I wonder if they know that some of us Reservists lost 7d a day of our pay when we were called up. We really lost it when we finished colour service, so some of us getting 4s 1d per week less than when we were serving. 'Twould be a sorry plight if we had stopped to wrangle over it, although our grievance in that respect is just as great, and perhaps greater, than theirs. Do we grouse and moan over it? No; of course not. We just think it over to ourselves, and keep thinking; that's all. Now, come on, you workers! You are working for the Government indirectly, and in many ways you have to help us, so you must keep the old flag flying, you know. And as for bonuses – well, we expect one as well when we come home, and if we don't get it we will all 'muck in' (Army slang) and divide up all the Iron Crosses we capture. You never know, they may be valuable some day. But don't let us read any more of refusing to work."

One person who became disillusioned with the war was the poet Siegfried Sassoon who had won the Military Cross and had been recommended for the Victoria Cross. In 1917 he wrote:

"I am making this statement as an act of wilful defiance of military authority, because I believe that the War is being deliberately prolonged by those who have the power to end it. I am a soldier, convinced that I am acting on behalf of soldiers. I believe that this war which I entered as a War of defence, has now become a War of aggression and conquest."

This cartoon in the 'Daily Mirror' highlighted not only the problem of drink, but also the apparent uncaring attitude of workers at home who were 'not pulling their weight'

CHAPTER 11

WOMEN AT WAR

Initially women's contribution to the war effort was confined to fund raising and helping Belgian refugees but in March 1915, with an increasing number of men joining the forces, there were serious labour shortages, particularly in the important munitions industry where new factories were being built to meet the huge demand for shells and ammunition. The Board of Trade urged women to take employment of any type and a Register of Women for War Service was introduced. The appeal was successful and women took all kinds of jobs, from office work to heavy industry. Prior to the war around 1,600,000 women had been employed in domestic service and most of these were young working-class girls. Most middle-class households employed a live-in maid, and the larger ones might employ a cook as well. Lower middle class households would have a daily or weekly maid, although she would not live with the family. A maid-of-all-work would earn anything from £8 - £16 per annum, depending on her age and experience. Live-in maids would have their food and a uniform provided which could add £25 a year to the family budget. By comparison a typist would expect to earn around £65 a year.

It is estimated that as many as 400,000 women left domestic service to take employment elsewhere; not only were they able to earn more and have greater freedom (many of them lived in hostels) but they were able to lead a more interesting life with contact with a wider group of people, including, of course, men. However, although women were working alongside men and doing the same jobs as them, their wages were by no means equal. The average man's weekly wage was around £3, a woman might be lucky to get a quarter of that. The Post Office was told by the Treasury that the maximum wage a woman could earn would be 25 shillings, although a skilled male worker's wage was £300 a year. The Post Office was also paying a war bonus to men of 2 to 3 shillings a week according to the wages, but women were given only half that amount. The employment of inexperienced women into the Post Office led to the introduction in March

Women took the place of the local postmen

1917 of the numbering of sub-districts, so the old London North district was divided into N1-N22 which made sorting of letters much easier.

On London Underground, around 50% of its male workforce was called up, creating many vacancies for women. On the buses nearly 60% of male staff was released for war service and tram operators suffered a loss of 29% of their men. The Trade Unions were initially resistant to women workers but were eventually won round when they were assured that the situation would only be temporary and the women would be paid the same rates as men. This meant that women did not start to appear until March 1916. Women working on cleaning and maintaining vehicles were supplied with dungarees whilst those acting as conductors on buses and trams wore relatively short skirts and leather leggings. Not surprisingly, the London General Omnibus Company (LGOC) found that 43% of their women workers had previously been domestic servants.

Women porters, guards and inspectors on the tube

Women working in the barrage balloon factory in the former Bohemia Cinema in Finchley Central

To give some idea of the importance of the role that women played, in 1914 there were 5,925,000 women in employment out of a population then of 45.4 million. By 1918 there were 7,103,000 - an increase of 19 percent.

As well as jobs in industry and commerce women had a role to play in the armed forces. Members of the Women's Army Auxiliary Corps (WAACs) were typists, cooks and telephonist and in the Women's Royal Naval Service (WRNs) they were signallers and maintenance workers. They also played an important part in the Women's Land Army, working on farms looking after livestock and planting crops, often in extremely arduous and harsh conditions. There was even a Women's Forestry Corps who felled trees and harvested the timber. As the war progressed and food shortages started to become a major problem, women's role on the land became even more important.

Miss M K McVeagh prepares to load up a water cart belonging to Finchley Urban District Council (photo LNA)

Women living in the countryside were also helping with the war effort. On 16 September 1915 in the small Welsh town of Llanfairpwll a group of local women met over cups of tea and home made cake and decided that they would try and help soldiers' families by growing vegetables, making jams and handicrafts. The idea caught on and by the end of the war there were 199 other Women's Institutes throughout the country.

Two local factories involved in war production employed many women. DeDion Bouton, a French company that before the war had made motor cars in its premises in High Road, North Finchley was producing gun parts while further up the road McCurd was making lorries. This factory closed shortly after the war and the premises were bought by H A Saunders who proceeded to buy and sell army surplus lorries and to strip them for spares. Initially he had one employee but he did well enough to become the Austin main agent for the district.

The McCurd lorry factory had a high percentage of women workers during the war   (photo Percy Reboul)

Women, of course, played a vital part as nurses during the war and one local girl is commemorated in St James's Church, Friern Barnet. Charlotte Henry was a Staff Nurse in the Queen Alexandra's Imperial Nursing Service. She died when the hospital ship *HMS Glenart Castle* was torpedoed by a U-boat ten miles west of Lundy Island at 4am on 26 February 1918. Among the 162 who perished were eight nurses, seven doctors, forty seven medical orderlies and the ship's captain. They, and 1800 others lost at sea and with no known grave, are commemorated on the Hollybrook Memorial in Southampton Cemetery.

One of the most bizarre stories of the war involving a woman was that of Dorothy Lawrence. Dorothy was born probably in 1888 and, having been abandoned by her mother was adopted by a guardian of the Church of England. She had an ambition to become a journalist, a rare occupation for a woman in the early days of the 20th century. She had a few articles published in *The Times* and at the outbreak of the First World War in 1914 she tried to become a war correspondent. Having been thwarted in this ambition in 1915 she went to France, managed to acquire a uniform and disguised herself as a man. She then managed to work her way into the Front Line and join the Royal Engineers 179 Tunnelling Company where she survived detection for ten days. She was eventually spotted, was detained in a French convent at St Loos and was court martialled. She was returned to England and wrote a book *Sapper Dorothy Lawrence: The Only English Woman Soldier* in 1919. She lived in Canonbury until 1925 when she claimed that she had been raped by her guardian. In what was almost certainly a cover-up she was declared insane and was committed to Colney Hatch Lunatic Asylum where she remained until her death on 29 August 1964.

Mabel Holman reported to her fiancée:

> "You ought to see England now; it's a funny old place – soldiers everywhere – there is such a scarcity of men that girls are doing the work – lifts in the shops, ticket collectors at the stations, driving vans. Some offices have nearly all girls now. F W & Co cannot get boys and seem to take a fresh supply of girls every day. S & H are having to send for some of the men to come back as, of course, the output is now as important as anything." *(16 June 1915)*

> "It is pretty terrible for girls these days – as usual they have to bear the brunt and it looks like most of them having to work for their bread and butter to the end of their days. They are taking men's places in all spheres now, and those who are left unprovided for, have a poor outlook in front of them. There are girls in the Bank tube ticket offices now – collectors, tube attendants. In fact it's a funny looking place London, not that they look funny – they are ten

times more polite and cheerful looking than the men." *(28 October 1915)*

"You would be surprised at the jobs girls are doing and the wages they are getting and I cannot see them ever giving this up. You can't get a servant for love nor money – both Mr B's have given him notice – one to go into a shop and another to be a postman. Another left to be a bus conductor, where they get £2 a week. We have milk girls, tube lift girls, bus and tram conductors, trades girls, telegraph girls. Even the post in the office is now delivered by a girl. Then in the higher grades they are doing munitions – running businesses – in banks and restaurants like Slater's, in fact, everywhere. I think it will be a tremendous problem and social revolution after the war." *(17 January 1917)*

The war came at a time when the suffragette movement was at its height and there were misgivings among their supporters whether they should support the war effort. In the 16 July 1915 issue of their newspaper *Votes for Women* the editorial stated:

"We continue to receive protests against the compulsory registration of voteless women. One correspondent asks us if we think it would be well for all Suffragettes to add to the form some such declaration as this: "As women have no vote, I don't intend to volunteer for any work until it is given." This correspondent mentions that she "would never lift one finger to obtain the vote by violence." Another Suffragette asks us if we favour the formula: "I am skilled enough to vote, and if I am worth registration, I am worth enfranchisement." We share to the full the passionate indignation which liberty lovers all over the country must necessarily feel at the compulsion of the voteless; we urged the Government from the first to do what only the Government can do – to remove, by the enfranchisement of women, the shame which is clogging the nation's progress. We warned the Government of the indignation they would arouse, of the harm they would do to the national unity. But we do not urge

Suffragettes to return any one specified answer under the Act, because we recognise the urgency in a time of national crisis, when so many of our best men are in danger, of the differences between the claims of one individual conscience and another. All Suffragettes are agreed in the desire to serve the best interests of the nation. Some – we need only mention the doctors – are directly helping in the conduct of the war; but many of the most passionately patriotic, who would give everything for their country, feel that they serve their country best by concentrating on the demand for a vote– by granting which, the Government would prove their boasted love of that liberty for which so many men are dying on the field of battle……All Suffragettes, whatever work they do as *individuals*, must continue to press for suffrage."

The divisions in the suffragette movement were mirrored in the Pankhurst family whose mother Emmeline had founded the Women's Social and Political Union in 1898. Despite her radical views, Emmeline considered that the threat posed by Germany was too great and she came out in support of Britain's stance on the war. Her daughter Christabel joined her mother in calling for support for conscription but her other two daughters, Adele, who had emigrated to Australia and Sylvia, who had become a committed socialist, were opposed. The split was so deep that Emmeline told Sylvia: "I am ashamed to know where you and Adele stand." For her part, Sylvia wrote to Adele in Australia and said of her mother and Christabel: "I only look in wonder and ask myself 'Can these two really be sane?'"

There is a popular conception that women's role in the war led directly to their getting the vote, however some historians contend that that had the war not intervened, they might have achieved this earlier because the suffragette movement had been a growing force for sixteen years and they had very nearly achieved their aims in 1912 but the Liberal Prime Minister, Herbert Asquith, changed his mind at the last minute and withdrew a bill that would have enfranchised them.

("My Magazine" April 1916)

(©IWM Art.IWM PST 5227)   (©IWM Art.IWM PST 5996)
Women were needed on the land and in the munitions factories

The Representation of the People Act of 1918 at last gave women over 30 the right to vote, however there was a caveat – they had to be either a member or married to a member of the Register. In the Act all men over 21 (except those who had registered as conscientious objectors) were given the vote, regardless of whether they owned property or not. Prior to this some 40% of men were too poor to qualify. As a result of the Act, some 8.4 million women were able to vote and the 1918 Eligibility of Women Act allowed them to be elected to Parliament. However, it was not until 1928 that all women earned the right to vote without any conditions.

With the increased freedom that women gained during the war, there came a gradual relaxation in some of the outdated Victorian restrictions. Divorces increased threefold, women started to frequent public houses, and they

The Lady Grocer

BEFORE the war we had 1,000 women in our employ, mainly engaged in clerical work. To-day we have nearly 3,000, and they not only do duty at the desk, but at the counter too, and all praise is due to them for the manner in which they have shouldered the extra burden.

¶ Their assistance has enabled us to release nearly 2,000 men for the army.

¶ Despite this enormous upheaval in our organisation, we are still able to satisfy our customers—a most ample tribute to the Lady Grocer.

INTERNATIONAL STORES

THE BIGGEST GROCERS IN THE WORLD
TEA :: COFFEE :: GROCERIES :: PROVISIONS

INTERNATIONAL STORES

Nearly 2,000 members of our male staff are in the Army, but we have a very able and willing staff of lady grocers ready to attend to your requirements

TEA COFFEE GROCERIES PROVISIONS

Advertisements in 'Barnet Press' in 1916

openly smoked in public. However, the most notable change was in women's fashions. Separate fashions for younger women had started to be introduced before 1914 so skirts had started to get shorter, in part because of the need not to have trailing skirts when in the workplace; a shortage of dress material was also a contributory factor. Advertisements for lingerie (known as "undies") began to appear in 1917, to the dismay of older women. Hair was cut short in bobs, again a practical move for anyone working in a factory. Women working in agriculture had to wear trousers and they would often wear these even when not working. In May 1915 the *Daily Mail* commented:

> "Just now our young and pretty girls are pushing the craze for short skirts to the utmost limit. But even now these ultra-remarkable

models are regarded with suspicion by women of good taste."

The streets of London were filled with young widows and bereaved mothers dressed in mourning and men, particularly young men, were noticeable by their absence. In fact there was hardly a family in the country that had not lost somebody in the war. It is estimated at there were 200,000 war widows and many of them suffered economic hardship, particularly as the pensions they received proved inadequate to support families. Others would have to look after disabled relations with little support from the state.

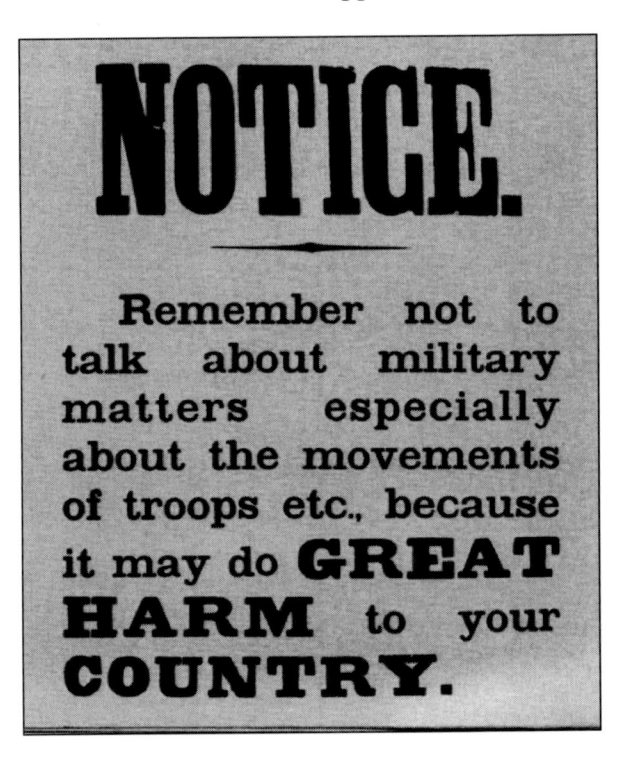

> **NOTICE.**
>
> Remember not to talk about military matters especially about the movements of troops etc., because it may do **GREAT HARM** to your **COUNTRY.**

A reminder not to gossip....

After the war women were again relegated to a secondary role in society and their contribution was soon forgotten. With the return of men from the front and the run-down of the munitions industry, women were dismissed from their jobs, often with as little as a week's notice. Not every woman wanted to return to a life in domestic service, although there were still jobs

BARKERS
of Kensington
LINGERIE SPECIALISTS

DAINTY PRESENTS

Barkers are showing a Charming Selection of the latest novelties in Dainty High-Class Lingerie.

Ladies have the choice of an unlimited variety of original and attractive styles at quite reasonable prices.

These garments are made in their own workrooms in exclusive styles of the latest vogue.

The illustration represents
THE "BLANCHE" COMBINATION, made of good quality Crêpe de Chine, handsomely trimmed Valenciennes Lace, with ribbon shoulder straps, and threaded ribbon at waist. In Ivory or Pink.

PRICE
23/9

Chemise to match, **15/11**
Knickers, **13/11**

JOHN BARKER & Co. Ld.
KENSINGTON HIGH ST.
LONDON · · W.8

Up to date fashions advertised in 'The Bystander' in 1917

(©IWM Q79964)

"Carry On!"

TYPES OF BRITAIN'S WOMEN ARMIES
Land Lasses, Town Toilers, and Sea Sirens

MAKE YOUR INVALID HAPPY IN A "VICTORIA" BATH CHAIR

LET him enjoy the health-giving air of heaven and the solace of society. A child can easily wheel him in his "Victoria" Chair, so he is not worried by giving trouble to others. The design of the chair is graceful and elegant. The self-guiding front wheel does away with "tilting" when turning, and a separate handle is supplied, attachable to the front, for use when the invalid wants to guide himself or prefers to be drawn.

This beautiful health-chair is fully described, as well as many other similar blessings for invalids, in No. 19 Album of Models. Post free for a post-card.

JOHN WARD, LIMITED
246, Tottenham Ct. Rd., London, W.
(Makers to their Majesties).

or **LEVESON & SONS**
(Incorporated with John Ward, Ltd.),
26, KNIGHTSBRIDGE, LONDON, S.W.;
35, PICCADILLY, MANCHESTER;
89, BOLD STREET, LIVERPOOL.

HAPPY THOUGH WOUNDED.

No More Crutch Paralysis.

Crutches with pneumatic head. Can be inflated with ordinary bicycle pump. Fitted on Patent Metal Adjustable Crutches, and the ordinary wooden type.

We are also makers of the Central Grip Crutch Walking Sticks.

Every Cripple should write for Illustrated Booklet.

THE MANSFIELD MOTOR BODY CO., LTD.
MANSFIELD, NOTTS.

Women were left to look after their injured menfolk

THE NURSES IN THE GREAT WAR.

HAVE *YOU* AS YET HELPED THE
NATION'S FUND for NURSES?

If not—can you think of a better cause for helping? The Nurses deserve all we can do for them. You agree—surely.

Read what the PRIME MINISTER said :

"*WE have included for the first time the mention of nurses, and nobly have they served; but not only have they been ministering angels in the hospitals behind the lines, but they have been constantly pushed forward to the casualty clearing stations only just behind the lines, and have actually stood between the living and the dead. Their names figure not only as heroines, but also as martyrs in this war. Several of them have been torpedoed and drowned at sea; several have been killed by bombs; and in one case a name has been rendered immortal by her martyrdom.*"

THERE is not a single soul in the Empire that does not feel a debt of gratitude to the Nurses in the Great War. They are magnificent. Yet, it will surprise most people to know that the Nursing Profession is without a complete organisation to help the Nurses in every way. That must be remedied. It can be. This Fund is arranged to do it. The cause is a noble one. The response we are sure will be worthy of the cause.

Please send a Donation to
THE VISCOUNTESS COWDRAY, Treasurer,
16, Carlton House Terrace, London, S.W. 1.

Full details of the Fund will be sent post paid on request to
THE BRITISH WOMEN'S HOSPITAL COMMITTEE,
21, Old Bond Street, London, W. 1.

Extract from the Hague Peace Conference held in 1907, to which Germany was a Signatory Power :—

Prisoners of War... Must Be Humanely Treated.

GERMANY has utterly failed to keep her part of the compact, and the testimony of our men who have been repatriated is that—

"But for the parcels sent from home we would have starved."

DO not forget our brave men who are prisoners of War, and who, during the trying months we are now entering into, will more than ever need our help.

Over 50,000 parcels have already been sent out by this Society, but more money is urgently required to meet the growing needs of our men.

Kindly send a donation at once to the
Rev. HUGH B. CHAPMAN,
7, Savoy Hill, London, W.C. 2.

The Royal Savoy Association for the Relief of British Prisoners of War.

Registered under the War Charities Act. Authorised by the Central Prisoners of War Committees.

What The Church Army does:

FOR THE MAN IN TRAINING
Recreation Huts, etc., in all the Training Centres at home and in France.

FOR THE FIGHTING MAN
Many hundreds of Recreation Huts, Tents, and Centres at home, in the shell area on the Western Front, at ports and bases in France, Malta, Egypt, Sinai and Palestine; Macedonia, Mesopotamia, East Africa and India, also a number for men of the Fleets at remote naval bases; Hostels in London for men on leave from the fronts; Kitchen Cars on the Western Front; Parcels for Lonely Men in Trenches.

FOR THE FIGHTING MAN'S WIFE AND LITTLE ONES
Hostels for Wives and Mothers Visiting Camps; Recreation Rooms; Free Treatment at Medical Mission; Holiday Homes; Care of Soldiers' Motherless Children.

FOR THE FIGHTING MAN'S PROVIDER—MUNITIONERS
Canteens in a large number of munition towns; Hostels and Rest Huts for Women Munitioners.

FOR THE PRISONER OF WAR
Parcels of Clothing and Comforts.

FOR THE WOUNDED MAN
Comforts for "Walking Wounded" in Huts, Tents, etc., close to the front; Friends for Wounded in Hospital far from own homes; Escort of Relatives to visit dying men in Hospital in France; Convalescent Homes for Wounded at seaside.

FOR THE DISABLED AND DISCHARGED MAN
Training for Work on Land at extensive Farm in Essex; Hostels for men while learning trade or seeking employment.

THE EXPENSE IS GREAT
Will you help to meet it? We must raise £100,000 within the next
VERY FEW MONTHS.

Charity appeals abounded

> "An Essential Garment for all Women Workers."
>
> BY APPOINTMENT TO H.M. QUEEN ALEXANDRA
>
> THE "Quorn Featherweight" Ladies' Service Waterproof
>
> Specially designed after the model of the celebrated "Quorn" Active Service Coat, for use when motor driving and for all other outdoor occupations. Absolutely waterproof and extremely light, with handy capacious concertina pockets and wind-cuff straps to sleeves.
>
> THE LADIES' "QUORN FEATHERWEIGHT" COAT combines SMARTNESS OF APPEARANCE with THE UTMOST SERVICEABILITY.
>
> PRICE £2 : 19 : 6
>
> Also supplied in heavy material.
>
> PRICE £3 : 18 : 6
>
> Only three measurements required :—Bust, Length of Sleeve from centre of back (arms bent) to length required, and height.
>
> **TURNBULL & ASSER**
> 71-72, JERMYN ST., ST. JAMES'S, LONDON, S.W.
> Telegrams: "PADDYWHACK, LONDON." Telephone: GERRARD 4628.

available; in fact there was a shortage of domestic staff. The Government and the public in general were unsympathetic and the general feeling was that women should not be taking jobs which could be done by men who had fought for their country. Married women were certainly not expected to be working; they were, after all, supposed to be supported by their husbands. As a result of these attitudes, by 1920 there were actually 2 percent fewer women working than in 1911.

The 1921 Census showed the extent of the change in society as a result of the war with there being a million and three quarter more women than men. The *Daily Mail* reported "The problem of two million superfluous women." One lady, Rose Harrison, summed it up in her autobiography *Rose, My Life in Service*:

"After the war men were scarce, the demand far outweighed the supply and a maid's limited and irregular time off was an added disadvantage. Then there was having to be back by ten o'clock which made every date like Cinderella's ball, only you didn't lose your slipper, you lost your job. There was no status being a servant, you were a nobody; marriage was the way out of it."

CHAPTER 12

FOUR MEN'S WAR

In December 1978 local historian Percy Reboul interviewed a survivor of the war, Ernest Davidson of East Barnet.

Ernest joined the Army at the age of sixteen in 1909 as a trumpeter, "the lowest form of animal life." He eventually became a gunner and by the time he had done four years in the Territorial Army he was looking for a change and wanted to join the balloon section at Westminster. One evening he was walking up Regency Street when he saw a notice saying 'London Electrical Engineers' and as there were some troops inside he went in to find out what it was all about. The sergeant-major there asked him if he wanted to join and what his trade was. When he said that he did not have a trade, he was told "Then you had better join the Second Fusiliers." On being told that he was already in the artillery and was just finishing his four years, the sergeant-major replied that they were allowed to bring in two or three non-tradesmen. Ernest signed up and found that he was with a lot of very highly qualified technicians, most of whom had been telephone managers and skilled electricians in civilian life.

The London Electrical Engineers consisted of four companies with about thirty men in each and they were mostly involved in what was called Coastal Defence, which involved being posted at all the fortresses around the country at Plymouth and Portsmouth, the Thames Estuary and as far north as Newcastle. They took up what was called Imperial Service. The ordinary territorials in those days only signed up for home service, but taking Imperial Service meant that they had other obligations and could be called out even if there was not a war on, or even the threat of war.

The basic soldier's pay was one and three halfpence a day which was supplemented by working pay which started of at fourpence a day at the lowest rank and, on the passing of an exam, would rise to eightpence. It then rose to a shilling with the top rate being one shilling and twopence.

On the day he was called up Ernest had just returned from lunch and about two thirty he received a telephone call and someone at the other end said: "Come up at once. Report to Regency Street" He replied: "I am at work, I can't do that." But he returned home and got into his Army uniform, went to Regency Street and was taken by lorry to Waterloo Station where he was put on a train to Plymouth. Ernest's boss was a Colonel in the Twentieth London and when he heard what had happened to his employee he rang his adjutant at Blackheath and said: "Have you heard about the Territorials being called out?" On arrival at Plymouth Ernest found that everything was fully equipped and operating.

Ernest was deployed with the Royal Engineers and one of their key roles was building bridges but on one occasion in 1915 in France he was introduced to the oxy-acetylene searchlight. This consisted of an oxygen cylinder and one of carbide which impinged onto a mantle which became white hot and the light was reflected off a silver mirror. The searchlight was mounted on a rod so that it could be poked over the top of a trench and illuminate No Man's Land to try and catch out any advancing Germans. Needless to say it proved completely useless as the first time it was used it received a hail of bullets from the German lines. The only time the searchlight was used thereafter was when they had concert parties and it would be stuck at the back of a barn! Searchlights were, however, later used successfully to track Zeppelins over London.

Ernest recalled that the French people welcomed the Tommies, but only because of the money they spent. Ernest initially worked at the docks in Rouen and had to go down at six in the morning and unload ships until eight o'clock at night. If they had the chance to go up the line they took it with both hands. Later on they were taken every day in cattle trucks to the front line, about ten miles away, where they were responsible for keeping things in repair. The dugouts were close timbered and sandbags were used to support the earth on the sides and Ernest was of the opinion that British trenches were not nearly as well constructed as the German ones which were magnificent.

Most of the troops were youngsters and although they did not enjoy the experience, there was a lot of friendship. Things got worse in July 1916 with the Battle of the Somme; Rouen was packed with troops and there were bodies all over the place and amputations were going on all the time. It was when he saw the hospital trains coming in that he realised that there was a real war on. There were over 60,000 casualties and bodies were just left in the fields and the stench was appalling and was exacerbated by the lack of proper sanitary accommodation. The worst part was at Ypres where the weather was so cold that the ground was frozen solid and stakes had to be put in with a sledgehammer. But without any warning a thaw took place and suddenly everything was changed to mud. On one occasion four or five men were in danger of sinking into the mud and they put out an SOS which Ernest's group answered. They got lengths of canvas and put strips of wood about every foot and these were bundled up and taken to the line. The device did not last long as it was very soon under mud, but it did enable the men to be moved to firmer ground. Mud was always a problem and it caused the death of many men. On one morning when daylight came Ernest realised that he had been standing on a dead body on which the clothing had rotted - it had probably been there for some months.

Despite the mud and continuous bombardment the thing that most men were afraid of was gas which was first introduced by the Germans in April 1915 at the Second Battle of Ypres. The first gas masks consisted of just a hood with a piece of mica across the eye hole and after two minutes or so the wearer could hardly breathe. The British retaliated and Ernest recalled that they took cylinders up to the line but when the gas was released the wind took it back into the men's faces.

Many of the experienced men in Ernest's company were sent back to England to help train Kitchener's Army, those inexperience men who had volunteered in the early days of the war, but Ernest was sent up the line with what was called an Army Troop Company which did the more permanent jobs such as looking after water supplies. There were two of them in charge of a pumping station for a considerable time which delivered perfectly pure water.

The soldiers, however, were not too careful about hygiene and would merely empty their tea cans and then fill them with water without cleaning them. In order to overcome this, chlorine was introduced into the water supplies and on a particularly memorable occasion an infantryman was instructed to put two spoonfuls of chlorine into a large water tank. The following day Australian troops who were not far away came and boiled up the water for their morning tea. They went on parade and soon one man had to run to the latrine, quickly followed by others. They knew that the tea had tasted funny but it was all they had. The Medical Officer came down and asked the infantryman how much chlorine he had put in. He replied that as he did not have a scoop he put half the tin in. He had thrown away the spoon, thinking it was just a piece of tin.

Ernest's billet was in the loft of an old farm and the occupants used to invite them down into the kitchen where the farmer's wife would give them soup which suited them even though it appeared to be made from nothing more than grass. They were very friendly, particularly their daughter who had led a sheltered life and who was suddenly the object of attention from twelve British soldiers!

Ernest recalled that he was never so fit in his life and strangely, although he had suffered from rheumatism before the war, he never had an occurrence while in France. At Passchendael, he was involved in building what was called a corduroy road which consisted of forest planking which was put down on top of wooden bearers and which was used to transport ammunition to the line. Some two hundred men were involved, two to a plank and the Royal Engineers would then construct the road. Unfortunately the Germans knew the exact range and two hundred yards of road would be destroyed in about four seconds.

A graphic illustration of the effects of gas

When he was transferred to Armentières the conditions were absolutely shocking and directly a hole was dug it immediately filled with water so sandbag walls were built, but even then there was always about two feet of water at the bottom of the trench and trench foot was a continuous problem as it could lead to gangrene and eventual amputation.

When asked for his view of the war, Ernest said that he felt they had no option but to fight and he did not see how they could have avoided it with the enemy coming against them and he certainly would not have been a pacifist. As far as the Germans were concerned he found that when he was working with prisoners of war they were all quite friendly and that they worked a damn sight better than the British!

Another London man had a completely different wartime experience and for very different reasons. Walter Daniel John Tull was born on 28 April 1888 in Folkestone and was of mixed race – his father was from Barbados and his mother was English. By the time he was nine both his parents had died and he was brought up in an orphanage in Bethnal Green. He was a talented footballer and cricketer and started his football career at Clapton where his form was described in 1909 by the *Football Star*; "…our dusky friend with his clever footwork is without doubt Clapton's catch of the season." Following a pre-season tour in May 1909 to Argentina with the Tottenham team he signed professional forms for them at £4 a week plus a £10 signing on fee. He made his league debut for them in September 1909 at centre forward where he had replaced Vivien Woodward who had been transferred to Chelsea. Altogether he played thirty first team games for Spurs and scored six goals but he was dogged by abuse from opposition supporters. In one match in particular, against Bristol City on 2 October 1909 the *Football Star* reported:

> "….he is Hotspurs' most brainy forward. Candidly Tull has much to contend with on account of his colour. His tactics were absolutely beyond reproach, but he became the butt of the ignorant partisan. Once, because he 'floored' Annan with a perfectly fair shoulder charge, a section of the spectators made a cowardly attack upon him in language lower than Billingsgate. Let me tell these Bristol hooligans (there were but few of them in a crowd of nearly twenty thousand) that Tull is so clean in mind and method as to be a model for all white men who play football whether they be amateur or professional. In point of ability, if not actual achievement, Tull was the best forward on the field."

After that game his first team appearances were few, although he played regularly for the reserves, making 27 appearances and scoring ten goals.

Walter Tull photographed during his time at Spurs

Walter was transferred to the Southern League team Northampton Town in October 1911. His career with them was more successful and he made 111 appearances and scored nine goals.

With the outbreak of war he enlisted in December 1914 with the Middlesex Regiment. On 18 November 1915 he was sent to Boulogne and in May 1916, after six months without leave, he was sent back to England suffering from 'acute mania.' or 'shell shock.' This was not uncommon among front line troops who had been subjected to continual bombardment in appalling conditions and it is estimated that around 200,000 soldiers suffered from psychiatric problems which led to their discharge from the Army.

After 5 months of recuperation Tull was posted to the 27th Battalion of the Middlesex Regiment at Mill Hill Barracks and then transferred to France on 20 September 1916 where he joined his battalion on the Somme.

He was sent back to England on Boxing Day 1916 where he underwent a four month officer training course which resulted in him being commissioned as a Second Lieutenant – the first ever black infantry officer in the British Army.

On 4 August 1917 he was posted back to France and on Christmas Eve of 1917 Tull led a raid under cover of darkness at Messines. This was the first recorded instance of a black officer leading white British infantry troops on a mission in wartime.

On 25 March 1918 Tull was killed in a defensive action on the Baupaume-Sapignes Road. One of his superiors, a Major Poole, said of him:

> "Tull was very cool in moments of danger and always volunteered for any enterprise that might be of service. He was recommended recently for a Military Cross. He had taken part in many raids. His courage was of the highest order and was combined with a quite and unassuming manner."

Second Lieutenant Pickard echoed the praise:

> "Allow me to say how popular he was throughout the Battalion. He was brave and conscientious. He had been recommended for the Military Cross and certainly earned it; the commanding officer had

every confidence in him and he was liked by his men. Now he has paid the supreme sacrifice pro patria; the Battalion and Company have lost a faithful officer; personally I have lost a friend. Can I say more! Except that I hope that those who remain may be as true and faithful as he."

Tull's body was never recovered and, along with 35,000 other missing men, his name is recorded on the Arras Memorial at Faubourg d'Amiens. Despite several attempts to have him posthumously awarded the Military Cross this has never happened.

One of the many unsung heroes of the war. Wilfred Smale, a woodcraft teacher at Woodhouse School, North Finchley, is fourth from the left in the middle row in this photograph from 1916. He was in the Royal Army Medical Corps (Percy Reboul)

Some men, of course, survived the war and went on to make worthwhile contributions in later life. One such man was Field Marshal Julian Byng (1862-1935) who was born in Wrotham Park just north of Barnet. He was a cavalry man who distinguished himself at Gallipoli, served as Commander of the Canadian Corps and finished as Commander of the 3rd Army throughout 1917 and 1918. In contrast to many other of the senior officers of the time, who were despised by the men, he was highly regarded by his soldiers for his robust common sense and ability to communicate at all levels. He took the trouble to explain his plans to his men and even on the eve of the Vimy battle in 1917 issued 40,000 printed diagrams to ensure that everyone knew their role. The ANZAC Chief of Staff, General White, said of him: "Byng was an unambitious man without any desire for personal fame – a very rare thing in Generals and a very precious quality in those under him."

Byng's life was devoted to the service of others, He was Governor General of Canada form 1921-1926 and Commissioner of the Metropolitan Police from 1928-1931. In 1923 he opened the East Barnet War Memorial.

According to the *Finchley Press* of 2 January 1919, Sergeant Albert William Baker of the 4th Battalion of the Middlesex Regiment was taken prisoner on 23 August 1914, which would make him the first soldier to be captured by the Germans. According to the regimental diary the 4th Battalion moved to the Mons-Conde canal on 22 August. Enemy shelling began over the night of 22 -23 August. Private John Parr was sent to reconnoitre the German positions and became the first British man to be killed in the war. During the afternoon of the 23rd the battalion was forced to retire towards Hyon and Nouvells.

Owing to the broken nature of the ground and the intensive German shelling, Sergeant Baker and two other men became separated during the early part of the retreat and were captured at about 10.30 am. When the roll was finally called on the 24th, six officers were reported killed and a further nine wounded. 453 other ranks were killed, wounded or missing. During the next two days over 200 stragglers reported for duty. Sergeant Baker was sent to Sennelager prison camp and notification of his capture was not received until 10 March 1915.

Sergeant Baker had enlisted at Mill Hill barracks on 12 February 1907, aged 18 and prior to that he had been a milk carrier for Manor Farm Dairies. His weight on enlistment was 110lbs, but regular army food sent him up to 128lbs after six months service. He was discharged from the army on 10 March 1919 and was awarded the 1914 star to his War and victory medals. He married Ellen Dove of 26 Stanhope Road, North Finchley and they lived at 3 Cecil Cottages, Rasper Road, Whetstone.

Baker caught chronic bronchitis as a result of insufficient nourishment and general ill treatment while a Prisoner of War and, after an examination at Barnet War Hospital (today's Barnet Hospital) was granted a pension of 6d a day more than the general disability pension. After a period of compassionate leave he was transferred to the reserve on 1 March 1919 and he retired from the Army on 31 March 1920 and lived on his pension at 7 Cecil Cottages in Rasper Road.

CHAPTER 13

TERROR FROM THE AIR

As if things weren't bad enough at home, the civilian population had to undergo something that had never been experienced before – being bombed from the air. This was a new departure in warfare as up until then armies had fought armies and civilians had not been involved, indeed women and children had generally been respected by the combatants.

The cause of the anxiety was the Zeppelin - a huge rigid airship consisting of a cigar-shaped envelope filled with bags of hydrogen and with gondolas suspended underneath in which the crew and the engines were housed. Because of their sheer size (they were over 500 feet long) they were extremely intimidating and as they were only able to travel at 50 miles an hour their looming presence made them more threatening.

The first realisation that things had changed forever came in January 1915 when a Zeppelin bombed Great Yarmouth and King's Lynn. On Monday 31 May 1915 London was targeted and raids continued across Britain in 1915 with raids on Ipswich, Southend, Dover, Hull, Tyneside, Ashford, Harwich, Deptford and Bermondsey. There were over a dozen further raids on Britain throughout 1915, with targets ranging from Hull and Tyneside to Southend and London. Casualties were comparatively light - 181 killed and 455 injured - but the damage caused was estimated at over £600,000.

Public anger at these raids forced the authorities to install counter measures in 1916. Searchlights often managed to pick out the raiders but anti-aircraft guns were largely ineffective due to the height at which Zeppelins operated. These measures did however help to boost morale with the feeling that at least something was being done.

Air raid warnings were instituted – a maroon was fired when the raiders were spotted and a bugle was blown to signify the all clear. As most of the Zeppelin raids were at night, the showing of any kind of light on the ground at night was considered to be of possible aid to them so a blackout was introduced. In July 1916 a Dr Fraser Nash of Oakdene Nursing Home, Oakleigh Road, Whetstone pleaded guilty for having a bright unshaded light at night and was fined ten shillings. At the same court hearing a man from Fortis Green was fined five shillings for a similar offence.

An air raid shelter in The Strand

Initially street lights were shaded from above but when it was realised that this merely threw pools of light on to the road, they were turned off altogether. The use of car headlights was also curtailed but one problem that could not be resolved was the arcing caused by the traction arms of trams in contact with the overhead wires. For this reason tram drivers were instructed to drive slowly and services were often reduced at night.

The Royal Flying Corps (RFC) had little success in attacking Zeppelins as their machines were slow and could not easily reach the 12,000 feet altitude at which the Zeppelins operated. When an RFC pilot managed to get in range of a Zeppelin the ammunition he had would pass right through the envelope without setting fire to it. Only later, with the introduction of incendiary bullets, were successes gained. There were no raids on London in 1916 until 24 August when the area around West Ferry Road was attacked with the loss of 9 lives and 40 casualties and with damage of £130,000. Beatrice Webb described her experience of the raids:

> "Six successive air raids have wrecked the nerves of Londoners, with the result of a good deal of panic even amongst the well-to-do and the educated. The first two nights I felt myself under the sway of foolish fear. My feet were cold and my heart pattered its protest against physical danger. But the fear wore off, and by Monday night's raid, I had recovered self-possession and read through the noise of the barrage with the help of an additional cigarette."

Siegfried Sassoon commented on a raid on Liverpool Street Station in September 1915.

> "This sort of danger seemed to demand a quality of courage dissimilar to front line fortitude. In a trench one was acclimatised to the notion of being exterminated and there was a sense or organised retaliation. But here one was helpless; an invisible enemy sent destruction spinning down from a fine weather sky; poor old men bought a railway ticket and were trundled away again dead on a barrow; wounded women lay about in the station groaning."

On the lighter side, local historian Percy Reboul's father described an air raid incident:

> "My father had been called up into the army and my mother had five children to `look after. We had air raids during the war, although nothing like those of the 1939-45 war. When the maroons went up

(the alert sign of those days) we used to go into the cellar of the Black Bull pub in High Road, Whetstone. One night, however, we went into a neighbour's house to wait for the 'all clear' to go. The

(©IWM Art.IWM PST 13660)

neighbour had a greyhound dog which was under the table. Suddenly there was a big bang and clouds of smoke – we thought we had been hit by a bomb and there was screaming and everyone went as white as a sheet. What had happened though was that the dog had got hold of a box of Swan Vesta matches, had chewed the box and caused the matches to explode!"

With the increase of air raids in London from July 1917 Underground companies allowed the platforms and passages at their stations to be used by shelterers. Initially these were meant for people who happened to be in the street at the time of an air raid but eventually they became used by anyone seeking refuge. As many as four and a half million people used the shelters on more than thirty occasions. At a local level it was reported in December 1917 that arrangements were well advanced whereby Holly Park Schools and the subway of the Great Northern Railway station, Brunswick Park, could be utilised by the public during the progress of air raids. At Palmers Green air raid warnings could be recognised by the hoisting of a red flag at the Council Offices during the day and a red light in the clock tower at night. The "all clear" signal would be a green flag in the day and a green light at night. There is no mention of how people living in other areas would be informed.

The first success in defeating the aerial threat came on 2 September 1917 when Zeppelin LS11 was attacked by three British BE2c planes and one pilot, William Leefe Robinson, managed to get off enough ammunition from his Lewis gun to set light to the gas bags. The airship fell to earth at Cuffley and there were no survivors. Leefe Robinson subsequently received the Victoria Cross.

On 1 October eleven Zeppelins set out to attack England and one of them, L31 captained by the ace pilot German Kapitanleutnant Heinrich Mathey, arrived over London from the north west. It was caught in searchlights and dropped 50 bombs over Cheshunt to lighten its load and gain height. Five Royal Flying Corps planes, one of them piloted by Leefe Robinson, were scrambled. On the ground, twenty-six year-old Second Lieutenant Wulstan

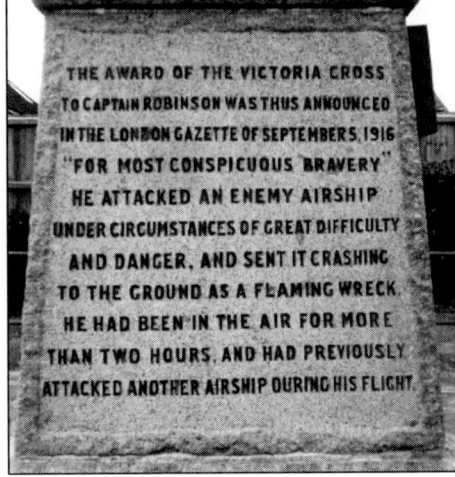

The monument at Cuffley to Leefe Robinson (Author)

Tempest was dining with friends when he received a telephone call ordering him to stand by. He was ordered to take off and patrol at 8000 feet over Central London, but he ignored the orders and decided to climb higher. Just before midnight he noticed one searchlight about fifteen miles to the north which was soon joined by five others and they were focussing on a Zeppelin which was beginning to lose height. With the anti-aircraft shells bursting around him, Tempest managed to gain height and found himself above the Zeppelin. He approached her from behind and fired three bursts, the last of which saw the inside of the envelope "go red like a Chinese lantern". He then described what happened next:

> "Flames burst from her glowing envelope and licked her bows. Brighter they grew, ruby, orange, yellow, paler. And then she seemed to be coming straight at me. I did a frantic nose dive with the burning wreckage tearing down on me. Only by putting my machine into a spin did I manage to corkscrew out of the way as the blazing mass everywhere in the sky. Far below that white-bright mass was receding, till a cloud of ascending sparks told me it had hit the ground."

The Zeppelin had fallen at Potters Bar and everyone on board was killed. Tempest visited the site the next day:

> "The blackened skeleton of the vanquished monster lay across two fields, and the enterprising farmer to whom they belonged was making a charge at the gate. I paid my shilling and went in."

Tempest was later awarded the D.S.O. Parts of the L31 can be seen at Potters Bar Museum to this day. The *Barnet Press* described the immediate aftermath:

> "Within fifteen minutes of the bringing down of the Zeppelin, every road converging on the spot where it dropped was thronged with pedestrians and motor traffic, and within an hour the village street, packed with brilliantly lighted motor-cars and cycles, resembled

A Zeppelin at its home base in Germany

The BE2c, one of the workhorses of the RFC

Piccadilly on a gala night rather than a sombre hamlet "somewhere in Middlesex". Within two hours at least forty motor-buses had arrived with military and police detachments, and long before that the military had taken charge of the wrecked airship and surrounded it with a three deep cordon of "Specials" and Volunteers to keep off the public……..half the people of Finchley turned out of doors when the Zepp burst into flames, and the cheering was such as to wake the soundest sleepers. The thing seemed to fall so near that thousands flocked along the main roads in the hope of picking up a relic. It is now a common thing for Finchleians to gather at nights at Tally Ho Corner and other places, waiting and hoping for another firework show."

The *Daily Chronicle* described a journey by people heading to Barnet Fair:

"People who intended making their yearly journey to Barnet contemplated the first part of their journey with honest intention. Then a voice in the train, bus or tram would ask: "Going to the Zepp? No? Well it's something I wouldn't miss. Nothing to see? Well that's as may be, but I'm not going to miss what's left anyhow." And so, almost at the last minute, the Fair-goers altered their mind and walked or trained to the little village in the hills of Hertfordshire."

The *Barnet Press* of 7 October 1916 contained a graphic description of the aftermath as seen by a member of the VAD:

"We watched the ship fall in a blaze of light, located the spot where it fell without much difficulty, and in about twenty minutes we reached the scene. During most of the time it was very dark in the field where the ship fell, and it was with the greatest difficulty that we were able to find the members of the crew. One of our men actually tripped over a German lying on the ground, legs and arms apart. In our practices we learned ambulance drill in the dark, and knew all about bandaging in the dark, so that the thought of dealing with cases in the dead of night in no way upset us. When we reached the scene we had practically a clear course, but soon the ground was overrun with sightseers and relic hunters. We found some members of the crew, who had evidently jumped from the ship, lying in different parts of the field, some many yards apart, and those were dealt with first. All the cases we took in hand were tall and well-built men. One of them was over six feet in height, and about 14 stone in weight. We could easily judge his height by the overlapping of his feet on the stretcher. The bodies were carried to the outhouse on the farm. There was no bandaging for us to do, but the lessons we had learned in stretcher work we put to practical use. A part of the time in the earlier stages we were assisted in our work by the glare of the fire in the ship, but when the fire died down we worked in absolute darkness."

Mabel Holman described the scene from her house in Muswell Hill:

"We had a raid last night and the huge excitement of watching a Zepp brought down in flames at Potters Bar – all in front of our windows. We saw the Zepps. Directly the searchlight found it and then for about 20 minutes it tried to escape by going higher, then twisting about. We knew an aeroplane (or planes) was after it. Then suddenly it was all alight – we saw the first shot from the aeroplane (looked like a Comet) but this missed, the second one set fire to it. It was an awful spectacle – our road was in darkness and intense silence, but directly the thing caught fire, everyone cheered and clapped. It was one vast roar - we yelled ourselves hoarse. The road was now lighted up bright red like a scene from Hades!!! The aeroplane signalled then by green and red lights (cease firing) and then I suppose went off – anyway what pluck of the fellow. This was not the end, as there was another about somewhere till about 2 this morning the searchlights were trying to find it, so you can guess we didn't get much sleep. As you know Potters Bar is only 4 or 5 miles from us, perhaps less than that as the crow flies. It was horrible to think of human beings were burnt to death. *(2 October 1916)*

There were stories of the Commander's waistcoat and parts of the fuselage being sold the next day in the area. Those hoping for another firework show were to be disappointed: after Potters Bar there were no more Zeppelin raids on London.

Zeppelins had featured in Mabel's letters from the onset of the war and her letters demonstrate their effect on the British population:

This poster may have helped recruitment but it can't have done much for civilian morale
(©IWM Art.IWM PST 12052)

An enterprising company offered air-raid insurance
('Bystander' 12 Dec 1917)

"Yesterday we had the airship over London. It is guarding us night and day. I did not see it but Mr Bowtell said it came right along Fenchurch Street and down Lloyds Avenue, travelling very low. When it got to the end of Lloyds Avenue it stood still and had a look round." *(21 September 1914)*

"London's lights are to be still lower – I think they must be expecting an aerial attack – I hope they won't come. It's foggy today. I expect they'll wait for the foggy weather to start." *(7 October 1914)*

"News just through that Germans are bombarding Scarborough and Hartlepool. I don't know any details yet. Sounds exciting, but I don't suppose they will do much damage. Probably kill a winkle." *(11 December 1914)*

"Boxing Day was a fearful night – wet and foggy and we felt rather afraid of Zeppelins as Xmas Day one (aeroplane) got to Sheerness and they threatened to come about Christmas – still nothing happened." *(21 December 1914)*

"A Special Constable in the City of London last night expected to be called out at any moment as there was an air-raid expected on London. Sure enough they got pretty close – Colchester, Clacton, Maldon etc." *(16 April 1915)*

"We shall have a warm time if the Zeppelins do come. They have threatened to set fire to London. The Special Constables have been called up today as they rather expect them, but we have had these scares before." *(16 May 1915)*

"Monday night, London was visited by Zepps – we were wakened by Special Constables being knocked up – then aeroplanes and then shooting. No account of places visited is to be given, but we have heard different people's experiences. They were seen over us – did damage at Dalston, Islington, Whitechapel (2 or 3 people killed),

Shoreditch and Bishopsgate, so you see they were "warm." Mr Bowtell was awakened by fire engines – a house was blown to bits at or near West Green and also Stoke Newington. None of us got up – wish we had now, but we didn't realise it and everybody thought we wouldn't disturb the other. I think the Alexandra Palace being full of German prisoners will probably save us. We all went to bed in fear and trembling last night armed with towels and jugs of water (to put out fires if they dropped poisonous gases. One thing I am not going to do is ride on tubes – we have heard from two different sources that they will do something to them and in two instances lately we have been turned out of trains as "something wrong." *(2 June 1915)*

"Germany says in a message that they reached "Finchley, one of the northern suburbs of London". They did a tremendous amount of damage at Islington. 4 people have been killed and I believe a number injured. It was a terrible night - roads full of shrieking people and houses on fire – they used incendiary bombs." *(2 June 1915)*

"Aeroplanes do go out to meet the Zepps, but if they brought down a Zepp over a town the explosion of the terrific amount of shells it carries would do more harm than the bombs they were able to drop, consequently they try to drive them out to sea and there chance doing for them." *(23 June 1915)*

"We have already got respirators and fill the bath up every night, sleeping with one eye open and one ear listening." *(1 July 1915)*

"Last night I have never seen such crowds of aeroplanes up at once, to and fro over our house and chasing one another behind clouds. I believe they were looking for one or expecting another raid." *(12 August 1915)*

"We have had another air raid. Paper says "Eastern Counties" but Leyton is where it was. I heard the bombs at 10.30 and all the "Specials" in our road were banged up. You remember Miss Boyton in Hilda's office. Her house was wrecked and she says 4 roads were ruined and that the casualties were very heavy. They had a night of terror – on the doorstep all night and thousands in the road. A night watchman was blown to pieces outside their door. They say the Zepp was so low that it was firing (the men were) with revolvers on the people in the roads! We have in consequence all got very nervous." *(19 August 1915)*

"Two raids in succession! Tuesday night we spent mostly in the hall, shivering with fright – the bombs dropping somewhere near awoke us. It seems Enfield is the nearest point, but some say they got nearer to Muswell Hill. A Constable told me in the night they were "not far off." Of course, it is not in the papers, but 56 casualties. Then last night we had a far worse experience. I had just got to the gate, having been to see Ida, when terrific firing was heard. We tore in, got the others out of bed and made for downstairs – we thought we were being bombarded. We all shook with fright and terror and on making for the back of the house; saw the most awful, but still grand, sight – a Zeppelin being fired on by our guns. The searchlights lighting it up made it look like a huge glow worm. It came right over and got behind some clouds, shots going in all directions and one seemed to hit it and it went up straight, tail down, and as it went right over us they seemed to lose sight until evidently it got away. Bit the sight! One has never seen such a thing, we were too terrified to open our windows, as we might get hit, but we had a full view of a most wonderful spectacle. The guns were terrific and it sounded like hell let loose. We arrived this morning to find Broad Street barricaded and nearly every window smashed – likewise Liverpool Street. The big buildings at the corner of Blomfield Street have not a single window left – a bomb was dropped just astride the station, fell on a motor bus and smashed up 6 people and they can only find the remains of the driver. We could see the hole of course, no one was allowed down the road alongside the station, leading to Finsbury Circus. The crowd was tremendous. Wood Street, Cheapside is also badly damaged and caught on fire. Holborn, we hear, is also badly damaged. Everyone seems to think we shall have them now every night, if we do, we shall all be reduced to jelly.

"I expect the Zepps will get cheeky and come in the daytime soon, especially as they go away in comfort. They had a fine trip around London and even far away districts. I hope they don't come – it is very terrible." *(21 October 1915)*

"I went on Saturday morning with Uncle E to see the Zeppelins at HAC Headquarters. The photos of the Zepps being brought down at Potters Bar are exactly as we saw it and must have been taken in the air. The exhibition was most interesting, they have two large marquees full of "remains" and thousands have been to see them. We went on the last morning of the exhibition and one of the most interesting things was the observation car and gondola – the rest is all in pieces – engines and petrol tanks all smashed up. Some of the aluminium framework was fairly well preserved, but only in bits. They had also a captured German aeroplane there. I should not like to have been in the observation car as it is impossible to stand up – one must either lie flat or in a crouched position." *(18 October 1916)*

"You ask if any damage is done by falling shells in the raids. I think so – one empty shell case fell through a house opposite Louie's – right through the bedroom and just escaped the man in bed. Everyone is warned to keep indoors to avoid falling shrapnel from our own guns and it is very foolish of people to court disaster while the raid is on. We always look out of the window and go out when it is all over." *(27 October 1916)*

"There was a Zepp raid last night on NE coast. Herbert has rushed in to say "2 down" I wonder if it's true. Fancy their coming on such a bitterly cold night, but it's worse for our airmen, as they have no protection, whereas those in the Zepp are, I believe, under cover and heated. You should have seen the smile on all our faces at the news." *(27 November 1916)*

An advertisement from 1916 with a Zeppelin theme

"While we were all crowing over some good news of Zepps being short down, a German aeroplane has been dropping bombs on London!! Did you ever hear anything so extraordinary? It was in the west end. I think there are about 9 people injured. This morning, however, we heard that the aeroplane was brought down by the French on its way back. The confounded cheek of the thing seemed to tickle everyone and took our breath away. These are stirring times." *(27 November 1916)*

The increasing success of the British defences against the Zeppelins caused the Germans to increase their efforts to find an effective replacement. They considered that by attacking Britain from the air, the RFCs fighters would be so preoccupied in defending the homeland that they would not be able to

The message on the back of this postcard from 20 September 1915 reads: "Many thanks for your letter. Thought you might like this view. The second bay window of the two shown on the right is ours. A lamp post outside the front gate. No Zeppelins brought down on English soil. Motor o'bus blown to atoms outside L'pool Street Station and our chaps on duty at Holborn that night went to the scene & extricated 16 dead bodies from the wreckage. They described it as a horrible sight. Letter later." It is interesting that it is addressed to King's Lynn, which was the second British town to suffer a Zeppelin raid.

attack Germany. The main problem facing the German Army Air Service was the lack of range of their aircraft which until late 1916 had restricted their raids on Britain to the Kent coastal towns of Deal, Dover, Faversham, Ramsgate, Margate and Sittingbourne. These raids had managed to kill only 20 people and injure 57 more so they were more of a nuisance than a threat. However the creation of two new bombers, the Giant and the Gotha, which could easily reach London and could operate at night, added a new dimension. The first use of the Gothas occurred in May 1917 when 76 civilians were killed in raids on the south coast. The first attack on London occurred on 13 June 1917 when 162 were killed and 426 injured in the East End.

Mabel Holman seemed to have been more affected by aeroplane raids:

> "We have had a nice old raid – bombs dropping around us. We heard as we thought an airship and thinking it was one of ours we went to investigate. I stood under the skylight to try and see and suddenly a terrific bomb – the whole place shook and we thought a good place to be would be to stand in the strongroom, but thinking it calmly I think it was worst. Then bomb after bomb crashed all around. As soon as it was over I dashed out and found the building next door but one hit. A cordon was drawn right round it and a motor bus was brought up and from the window we watched most awful and harrowing scenes. Several dead bodies were brought out, girls I believe. It was awful to see relatives from other offices flying around to see if their dear ones were safe and their agony when they were told otherwise. *(12 June 1917)*

> "Our nerves are terribly shattered. Saturday's air raid was dreadful and bombs were dropped all around us - all our windows are smashed and we narrowly escaped injury from falling glass. One went through offices next to H and several in the same road, also each end of our avenue – the place is a sight. We had an alarm and stood waiting for one to come to us, then one went in the road just behind us, glass falling on to our skylight. We dashed into Mr B's

room and one went in front – they were trying to make me sit in his big green chair but I refused and pushed backwards just as windows and glass door came in. We none of us expected to come out alive. We would do anything to get out of town. We went up on Monday and each day had more alarms. We live in a state of terror and each day is a nightmare. To make matters worse Mother phoned to say a memento had been dropped in our garden – we had a police guard all the weekend and most people thought it was an aerial torpedo, however, on Monday night the military came and said it was a shell from our own guns and probably partly or wholly exploded and that there was no danger and that the police need not wait, for which we were profoundly thankful, although they were some of the nicest men possible and they would remove it as soon as possible. Several of these were dropped on the district and you can imagine the awful fright and escape that Mother had. Strange to say she didn't know at first it was in her garden – heard the dreadful crash when she was in the hall. She got the glasses and proceeded to watch the Germans – about 25 she counted – coming over in perfect formation. *(11 July 1917)*

"On Tuesday night we had a night of terror, up from 12 o'clock to 2.00am shivering with fright in the hall. It was diabolical and hideous though nothing was nearer than a mile or so away, but the awful firing and the noise of their engines getting nearer and nearer sent us all nearly silly. Then it was calm for a little while but we soon heard them returning and this happened three times. They crossed somewhere right over us and the drone of the machines and to see nothing is horrible and, of course, we expected the house to collapse on us at any minute. Then the next morning when I got to town there was another scare and everyone stampeded in the cellars but it was evidently only a false alarm. Of course, what we are really suffering from is shellshock of a sort and it will be impossible for civilians to go on working under these conditions" *(6 September 1917)*

> "We had a nice old raid on Monday night. 5 hours of it and a shower of shrapnel. I picked up several pieces within a foot of our windows; the firing was heavy but no damage in our immediate vicinity, other than from shrapnel shells from our own guns. They reached the centre of London and there are many casualties. Last night they started again and we had some more hours under fire but I see from the papers they didn't penetrate London defences, but all the guns were going and our corner was pretty noisy all the time. We have been up 2 nights now till 2 o'clock. We stand in the little well which is the entrance to the kitchen behind the stairs; it is away from glass - that is all you can say for it." *(28 January 1918)*

Another local resident had memories of aeroplane raids. Ena Constable, who was fifteen at the time and lived in Whetstone, described one particular raid:

> "I remember the bomb in Burleigh Road which demolished buildings and the house where Harry Vardon lived was caved in half by the bomb. My father was the principle air raid warden attached to the police station which was then in the High Road and he was always the first one to be called out when there was an alert. I can remember the daylight raid on 7 July 1917 when a whole lot of German aircraft came over and I remember their coming straight towards us and my father went out on duty having pushed my mother and I under the stairs and the wind changed and they veered over and dropped their bombs on Walthamstow, which was lucky for us."

Initially the Government's attitude to air raid warnings was a strange one as it was felt that sirens or hooters would only cause panic on the streets and would also interrupt war production. In fact, many Londoners went out on to the streets to watch both Zeppelins and, later, planes, rather than scurry for shelter.

Although not caused by an air-raid, there was a massive explosion at Silvertown in East London on 19 January 1917 when fifty tons of TNT exploded at a munitions factory. The blast killed 73 people and injured 400 and was heard over 100 miles away. Mabel Holman gave details to her fiancée:

> "The explosion was terrible; we had a fright here and thought it was at the end of the road. The house shook, windows were broken in the vicinity. Of course, we guessed it was not Zepps, although heaps thought it was and one lady came along the road in a state of collapse. Win was in town and she felt deaf when she got home. Windows are, of course, smashed in the City and you can imagine the extent it was felt when I tell you that Hilda was in a shop in the Broadway at Crouch End and the rush of air which preceded the explosion blew open the doors and sent goods flying and this is a good ten miles away." *(24 January 1917)*
>
> "The fellow in the next bed to him was ¾ of a mile away from the explosion and has lost a leg." *(28 February 1917)*

By the end of the war aeroplane raids had killed 959 people and injured 2267 while Zeppelins had accounted for 722 dead and 1815 injured. These figures were, however, dwarfed by the loss of life due to an influenza epidemic which occurred between March 1918 and the spring of 1919. Its origins are unclear although it may have started in China but the first reported cases were in Fort Riley in the USA. It spread rapidly throughout the world and since Spain was the first country to publicly announce the epidemic it became known thereafter as Spanish flu. Influenza normally attacks the frail and the elderly but this strain was so virulent that even young and healthy adults were affected. It has been estimated that half of the world's population was affected and the death toll worldwide was 40 – 50 million with deaths in Britain amounting to 228,000.

CHAPTER 14

THE END

By 1917 moves were being made which would lead to the end of the war. The Pope had tried to act as a middleman in diplomatic moves for a peace but his attempt failed. American President Woodrow Wilson had asked the combatants to give their aims for a settlement – 'peace without victory' but again this led to nothing.

America finally entered the war in 1917 and this was largely the result of a telegram that had been sent on 17 January 1917 from Arthur Zimmerman, the German Foreign Secretary to his ambassador in Mexico:

> "We intend to begin on the first of February unrestricted submarine warfare. We shall endeavour in spite of this to keep the United States of America neutral. In the event of this not succeeding, we make Mexico a proposal of alliance on the following basis: we make war together, make peace together, generous financial support and an understanding on our part that Mexico is to reconquer the lost territory in Texas, New Mexico, and Arizona. The settlement in detail is left to you. You will inform the President of the above most secretly as soon as the outbreak of war with the United States of America is certain and add the suggestion that he should, on his own initiative, invite Japan to immediate adherence and at the same time mediate between Japan and ourselves. Please call the President's attention to the fact that the ruthless employment of our submarines now offers the prospect of compelling England in a few months to make peace.   Signed ZIMMERMAN"

The telegram had been intercepted and decoded by British Intelligence and forwarded to the Americans. The contents invoked fury in America and on 6 April 1917 the USA declared war on Germany.

In Europe, Tsar Nicholas II abdicated on 15 March 1917 and he and his family would later be murdered on 16 July 1918. On 7 November 1917 the Bolsheviks overthrew the Russian government and on 29 November an armistice between Russia and Germany was signed. On 30 September an armistice was signed by the Allies and Bulgaria and on 17 October between Italy and Austria-Hungary.

As a result of the truce between Russia and Germany, German troops were able to be moved from the east to the western front but despite some notable advances into Allied territory the arrival of fresh and well equipped American soldiers tilted the balance in the Allies' favour and it soon became obvious that Germany would at last be defeated. Tensions arose between German politicians and the military who were insistent that there should be no surrender of German sovereignty over Alsace and Lorraine. A series of Allied counterattacks saw the retreat of the German army on 8 August and it was then, when there were mass desertions of German troops and the surrender of both Bulgaria and then Austria that Germany finally realised that the victory could never be won. There were riots on German streets and troops were attacked by civilians. On 9 1918 November Kaiser

Wilhelm abdicated and at 5.00am on 11 November the armistice was signed, with the cease fire taking place at 11.00am. On the front line Ernest Davidson recalled how he learned of the end of the war:

> "About two days before we were working on a trestle bridge because the Germans were retreating very fast at this time. It took 22 hours to put up this bridge. The artillery officer demanded that his troops would go over even before we had finished it. The first lot went over but the bridge started tilting and we stopped the rest going over. We went to a place near Mons to work on a much smaller bridge and on the following morning for some reason there seemed to be no life and we weren't told abut 10 o'clock when an officer came along and said "All right, you can pack up now – go back to your billets. It's the finish" and it was then that we learned that the war was over. This came as a tremendous shock to me and I walked for miles, absolutely stunned. After all this time the whole lot was over. I began to wonder, what was I going to do back in civvy life as I didn't want to go back into the job I left, it was too uninteresting. Most of us were just wandering about really, not a scrap of excitement. We went into then town and where the drink came from I do not know but I've never been so paralytic in all my life. One vivid memory, when I went back into the garden and it came out of me from every possible part….it was the same with everybody else, there was no discipline at all, nobody worried. We tried to recover the next day. That was my memory of 11 November 1918."

In Barnet the Rector hoisted the Union Jack above the tower of the parish church and the bells were rung. Shopkeepers put out flags and bunting and at 11.00 maroons were let off at the police station. From noon onwards shops closed and throughout the afternoon, despite persistent drizzle, people filled the High Street and a band played patriotic tunes. To round things off, a full sized cartoon of the Kaiser was ceremoniously burned. Similar scenes took place in Finchley and special services were held at Christ Church, St Paul's, St Barnabas, the North Finchley Congregational Church and

Ballards Lane Wesleyan Church. In Friern Barnet, however, a resident was surprised to see little sign of celebration:

"I walked from Bowes Park to the Orange Tree expecting to see displays of gratitude everywhere, but one would have thought it a place of mourning – not one light and only a few flags from windows here and there. Overhearing there was a house looking lovely in Holly Park-road, I made my way back to fond the 'one house' in the district that showed loyalty to our good lads, and turning from a dark byway came into full view of it. The number I noticed was 88. The whole front was lit by fairy lights, showing flags of all taking part in the fighting, and in the window was a silk

The railway carriage in which the Armistice was signed

banner representing England, Italy and France artistically draped with small flags. I raised my hat as I read 'God Bless Our Boys' and

I did thank God that peace had come at last and, and felt that our sons would be returning, and that those occupants had, like me, someone near and dear to them out there in the battlefield."

The *Finchley Press* reported the celebrations in Central London:

"As our representative was walking from Drury-lane to Fleet-street there was nothing to attract attention, everybody seemed bent on the particular business they had in hand, when suddenly the bursting of a maroon produced a wonderful transformation scene. It was the signal for everybody to "down tools," and less than a minute afterwards everybody was out in the street. The second maroon was received with waves of ear-piercing cheers that increased in volume with each succeeding maroon fired, until the whole City seemed to be one excited cheering crowd. The streets were quickly thronged, each business house pouring out its hive of busy workers, and it was surprising where the thousands of people had come from in so short a time. Men in their shirt sleeves and aprons, girls in their overalls and hatless, tradesmen and their assistants, employers and employees were there fraternising, while soldiers were everywhere. It was a laughing, cheering, merry, jostling throng.

Another surprising feature was where all the street flag-sellers had sprung from, and soon most people were displaying flags. The girls in their overalls, being hatless, stuck the flags in their hair. Work was abandoned and business suspended, while the bells of St Paul's, St Martin's and other churches rang out merry peals and then "fired." As time proceeded the wave of enthusiasm grew in intensity, and the munition girls were everywhere the leaders of their rejoicing. Soon the vehicular traffic became hopelessly congested and got beyond any police control. Taxis, 'buses, motor lorries, motor cars and horsed vehicles were wedged in by tens of thousands of jubilant men and women. At times it was impossible for the vehicles to move. 'Buses were boarded for joy rides. Army motor lorries were packed with soldiers and munition girls, laughing, cheering, shouting and thoroughly happy and perfectly oblivious to appearances. The noise was deafening amid the bells, the hooters, trumpets, the banging of the enamelled advertising boards outside the 'buses with sticks, and at one spot, tin trays, used as paper receptacles, were banged with ebony rulers at the first floor windows, while "flappers" and youths in the Government offices tore up forms and used them as confetti, with the result that the thoroughfare was strewn with paper for a considerable distance. The scene was a never to be forgotten one."

On Sunday 17 November thanksgiving services were held in local churches of all denominations. At Barnet Church the Rector said: "the news of the signing of the armistice lifted from all minds a horrible nightmare whilst the whole universe exclaimed: 'Thank God.'"

Whilst everyone was glad the war was at last over, there were those who could not bring themselves to join in the celebrations. People who had lost loved ones in the last months of the war must have been particularly bitter that it had not ended earlier. Mabel Holman wrote to her fiancée on 19 November 1918:

It's all over! Celebrations in Central London

"The Peace news was very disturbing to us. We all felt very ill and depressed and how people could go mad with rejoicing is beyond my comprehension. I really went mad with agony; however, I think other people's feelings might have been considered. The cost has been too great all round for such "Maffeking" scenes. We have, of course, absented ourselves from it all and none of us even went out of our offices to hear a cheer or see the crowds. We left it to those who have suffered no discomforts or losses through the war."

Some six weeks later it was Christmas. There was scarcely a home that had not known someone who had been killed or injured in the war. The mood was more sombre than celebratory. At that remote period Christmas was still a religious festival. The *Barnet Press* said:

> "The reappearance of the waits (carol singers) is reminiscent of pre-war times but it will be generally agreed that the quality of carol singing is not what it was before the war." We do not refer to the juveniles who go round murdering old world carols or more modern popular sings, but the properly organised singers. Where are the violins and cornets and portable harmoniums? Still it is pleasant once more to hear the familiar melodies warbled round the streets."

There were appeals for money for the Blinded Soldiers and a Children's Fund which raised over a thousand pounds. The Finchley Voluntary Nurses' fund also appealed for money because it was nearly bankrupt and again nearly a thousand pounds was raised. Another charity, the Middlesex Prisoners of War Fund, helped those who had suffered financially.

On a less happy note, the relatives of James Weir of Etchingham Park were told on Christmas morning that he had been killed on 16 October. Henry Holden of Lodge Lane, North Finchley had been killed a week before the Armistice, on 4 November. Of those returning, William Laurie of Finchley Park was released from German prisoner of war camp where he said that he had been well treated and had received Red Cross food parcels. Privates Mantle and Broughton, who had been captured in 1916 on the Somme were also returned. William Crosby, a builder, put an appeal in the paper: "I have lost touch with several of my employees and will be glad if they will get in touch with me."

Shops started to return to normal and Messrs. Hall & Co, drapers, in Whetstone High Road were open until 7.00pm on Christmas Eve and reopened at 9.00am on Boxing Day morning. The staff of Priors department store in North Finchley worked on Christmas Day preparing for the Boxing Day sale.

When statistics were compiled after the war the true horror of it all became apparent. In Europe 16 million had died of whom 995,939 were British (2.1% of the population) and of this total 109,000 were civilians. More than 35% of German men between the ages of 19 and 22 were killed and over half of French men between 20 and 32 were dead by the time the war was over. Some 2,272,998 British troops were wounded. The carnage was not confined to land – the British lost 5282 merchant ships to German U-boats.

Two battles were particularly bloody. At the Somme 177,739 British and Commonwealth soldiers were killed or wounded or were reported as missing. Of these 15,000 were killed and of the 90,000 missing a large number were taken as prisoners of war. In the first day alone 30,000 were

('Barnet Press 20 Nov 1918')   ('Barnet Press' 7 Dec 1918)

wounded. Passcehndaele in 1917 was a futile campaign where virtually no ground was gained and there were over 244,000 casualties. In the course of the war some 700 million artillery and mortar rounds were fired on the Western Front alone. It is a sobering thought that over 400,000 soldiers have no know resting place and even today French and Belgian farmers are turning up their remains which are then given a proper burial.

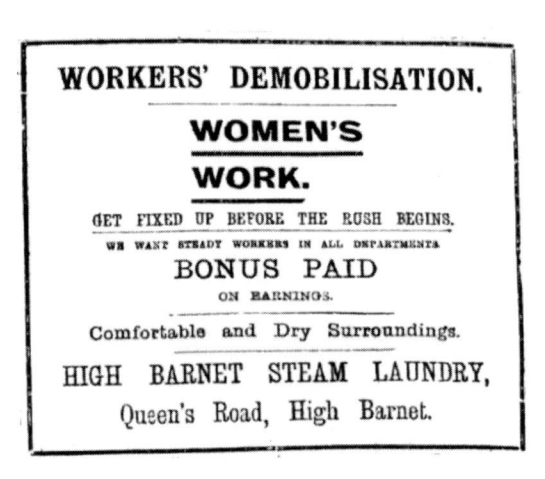

WORKERS' DEMOBILISATION.

WOMEN'S WORK.

GET FIXED UP BEFORE THE RUSH BEGINS.
WE WANT STEADY WORKERS IN ALL DEPARTMENTS

BONUS PAID ON EARNINGS.

Comfortable and Dry Surroundings.

HIGH BARNET STEAM LAUNDRY,
Queen's Road, High Barnet.

('Barnet Press' 23 Nov 1918)

WARD'S Great Victory FURNISHING SALE

Commences WEDNESDAY NEXT, 1st January.

Wonderful Bargains in High-grade Furniture, Bedsteads, Bedding, Carpets, Linos, Rugs, Household Drapery, Blankets, Quilts, Furnishing Ironmongery, China, Glass, Cutlery, Plate, Leather Goods, and everything appertaining to the Home.

£60,000 STOCK to be cleared regardless of cost.

A return to boring normality.
('Barnet Press' 26 Dec 1918)

CHAPTER 15

THE LEGACY

Demobilisation took a long time and did not start until December 1918. A soldier was first sent to a dispersal station where he collected a railway warrant, a ration book, a clothes allowance of 28 shillings or a 'demob' suit, and 28 days home leave. A Certificate of Employment was issued to every soldier; this gave details of what he had been doing in the Army and was meant to help him get back into employment. He was also given a Silver War Badge confirming that he had served his country honourably and had been discharged. Unemployment pay, for a period of thirteen weeks, was 24 shillings with 6 shillings for a child under fifteen and 3 shillings for each additional child. After 28 days the soldier would be considered demobilised although he was still held "in reserve" which meant that in the event of another war he could be called up again. Those seriously wounded or who had a disability were granted a war pension, the amount of which depended on the severity of their injury.

An editorial in *Barnet Press* in November 1918 highlighted the problems that faced the country after the euphoria of the armistice:

> "After a week of unrestrained rejoicing, the nation will have to settle down to deal with great problems - the demobilisation of the Army and munitions workers and the settling of them into civilian life. Where places have been kept open men returning will displace their replacements and the brave fellows returning from the front must have every consideration. Nevertheless the munitions workers from the De Dion works at Finchley will need special consideration as most of them are women and many are war widows."

On 13 December 1918 a number of workers from De Dion at High Road, North Finchley demonstrated at the offices of the Board of Works requesting equal treatment as was granted to other firms doing Government work. Around 600-700 workers attended and there were animated scenes at both Finchley and Whetstone as people collected for the long tram journey to Whitehall. The deputation was received and was listened to sympathetically. Before the deputation was received the crowd chanted 'We don't want charity.' A decision was made to keep the factory open until the New Year to ensure that Christmas wages would be paid.

No attempt was made to help find employment for ex-servicemen – they were left to their own devices and those who had been in the forces longest were more likely to be unemployed as they would tend to be more out of touch with their former employer than someone who had only recently been called up. One of the saddest sights after the war was ex-servicemen, both able bodied and wounded, reduced to begging or selling matches on the streets or, more disturbing, selling their medals for a pittance. One Whetstone resident remembered the problems with employment:

> "When I was demobilised after the 1914-18 war there were thousands of men thrown on the labour market. When you went to get a job, and I went to dozens and dozens for miles around, there would be up to 200 men waiting to be interviewed. For 10 months I lived on my gratuity, and then an uncle asked me why I didn't go to Scotland Yard and join the police. It was the last thing I thought of! I passed my exam and within a fortnight I was on Wellington Barracks doing footdrill again under a police drill sergeant: this was after doing drill for four or five years in the Army!"

A Finchley man confirmed the problem:

> "In those days most recruitment was through ex-servicemen and many postmen had served in the 1914-18 war. I applied for a job while I was in the Army and was put on a register. Two and a half years later a vacancy occurred."

The length of time taken to demobilise resulted in demonstrations in Whitehall by frustrated soldiers wielding placards: "We won the War. Give us our tickets", "We want civvies suits" and "No more red tape" The protestors were supported by the national newspapers and public opinion to such an extent that Winston Churchill was put in charge of demobilisation and he quickly got rid of the backlog by increasing the rate of discharge to 50,000 a day.

The slogan "Homes Fit for Heroes" sadly did not result in a massive house building programme and it was estimated that there was a shortage of some 600,000 homes as little building had taken place for four years. The situation was exacerbated by landlords evicting tenants in order to sell the properties to owner-occupiers. The Government tried to solve the problem by offering subsidies to private builders and also to local councils to enable them to build council houses but the housing shortage continued until the early 1930s.

Having experienced the horrors of the war, many returning soldiers were rightly critical of many aspects of the way it had been conducted, particularly the Army leaders who had led thousands of men into pointless battles that gained nothing. In the biography of one soldier *The Last Fighting Tommy* published in 2009, Harry Patch described his feelings on returning home:

> "By the time I was demobbed I was thoroughly disillusioned. I could never understand why my country could call me from a peacetime job and train me to go out to France and try to kill a man I never knew. Why did we fight? I asked myself that, many times. At the end of the war, the peace was settled round a table, so why the hell couldn't they do that at the start, without losing millions of men? I left the Army with my faith in the Church of England shattered. When I came home I joined the church choir to try to get the faith back, but in the end I went because I enjoyed the music and had friends there, but the belief? It didn't come. Armistice Day parade – no. Cassock and surplice – no. I felt shattered, absolutely,

and I didn't discuss the war with anyone from then on, and nobody brought it up if they could help it."

On the Home Front things took some time to get back to normal. Meat continued to be rationed until November 1919 and butter and sugar until 1920 and coal was still in short supply. Prices generally rose by some 75% although wages had risen on average by 100% since the beginning of the war. Manual workers weekly wages were as follows:

	1914	*1919*
Bricklayer	£2 2s 10d	£3 19s 2d
Labourer	£1 9s 1d	£3 5s 2d
Riveter	£1 17s 9d	£3 14s 9d
Compositor	£1 16s 0d	£3 12s 0d
Engine driver	£2 2s 0d	£4 10s 0d
Agricultural worker	13s 4d	£2 2s 0d

With the Treaty of Versailles on 28 June 1919 Germany was, among other things, made to pay over £6 billion to the Allies in reparations and to return Alsace and Lorraine to France. Article 231 firmly put the blame on Germany and her allies:

> "The allied governments affirm and Germany accepts, the responsibility of Germany and her allies for causing all the loss and damage to which the allied governments and their nationals have been subjected as a consequence of the war imposed upon them by the aggression of Germany and her allies."

An important part of the treaty was the setting up of the League of Nations which was later replaced by the United Nations.

An unintended consequence of the Treaty was the sense of injustice felt in Germany, particularly the amount that had to be paid to the allies. In fact it was impossible for them to meet the terms in full and it was this which was exploited by Adolf Hitler who, twenty one years after the end of the First World War, dragged the world into a second one.

With the passage of time, the full futility of the war came to be realised and was best summed up in a song popular in 1922:

> "We won the war, what was it for?
>
> You can ask Lloyd George, or Bonar Law.
>
> We beat the German, the Austrian and Turk
>
> That's why we're all walking round out of work.
>
> We won the war, what was it for?

But the next time the enemy's at your door

Take him in and shake his hand, Give him a dinner and treat him grand.

What's the use of fighting any more?"

Of all the poems that were written about the Great War, perhaps the most moving was that by a Canadian surgeon, Lieutenant Colonel John McCrae, who had treated casualties at the Second Battle of Ypres in 1915:

"In Flanders fields, the poppies blow

Between the crosses, row on row,

That mark our place; and in the sky

The larks, still bravely singing, fly

Scarce heard amid the guns below.

We are the Dead. Short days ago

We lived, felt dawn, saw sunset glow,

Loved, and were loved, and now we lie

In Flanders fields.

Take up our quarrel with the foe:

To you from failing hands we throw

The torch, be yours to hold it high.

If ye break faith with us who die

We shall not sleep, though poppies grow

In Flanders fields."

In July 1919 the Government announced that there would be Public Day of Thanksgiving on 6 July followed on Saturday 19 July by a day of national rejoicing. Peace Day celebrations took place in the area; the *Barnet Press* described what happened in Friern Barnet on the Saturday:

> "Two thousand happy looking children from all the elementary schools in Friern Barnet marched in procession on Saturday afternoon, from the Council Office to Friary Park. They were headed by a band, a real band, which caused the junior members of the great procession to feel unspeakably proud. The little ones looked for all the world like little Peter Pan soldiers on a joy march. They were in full war paint Oh, yes! Identity tickets, bearing their very own names, were pinned or sewn in the neighbourhood of their little hearts, and each and every protagonist was armed with a mug. Their faces lightened with almost every beat of the big drum and their eyes were full of optimistic wonder in regard to the good things that were to come. For this was Peace Celebration Day. Proudly these happy little people waved their hands to mother who was walking on the footpath like an ordinary human being; and now and again, led by big boys and big girls they sang spasmodic selections of 'Here we are Again' and 'Britons Never Shall be Slaves.' All went as merrily as a marriage bell until the rain began to fall ever so slightly but enough to make mother anxious. The children did not seem to care; in fact the boys appeared rather to enjoy the occasional showers. At last the dauntless marchers reached Friary Park, Here myriads of workers had been hard at work all day…..fixing up arrangements and entertainment for 2000 children is no joke. An excellent tea was provided and it was a pleasure to see the infants eating under the trees partaking of tea and cake in picnic fashion. But it was not all eating and drinking. There were sports with hordes of prizes. The number of events was known to no man, nor can anybody on earth say who were the winners. The runners were sorted into groups of four or five and the winner of every group received 1s 6d while the second pocketed 9d. It is sad to relate that the later festivities were marred by an almost continuous downpour of rain. Still the committee stuck to their

programme, the band continued to play and at the close of the day we had fireworks and a bonfire which lit up the district for miles around."

There has been criticism of the generals on both sides for needlessly causing so much carnage in the pursuit of a gain of a few hundred yards of ground. An article by Sir Douglas Haig written in 1926 perhaps shows how out of touch with reality they were:

"I believe that the value of the horse and the opportunity for the horse in the future are likely to be as great as ever. Aeroplanes and tanks are accessories to the man and the horse, and I feel sure that as time goes on you will find just as much use for the horse – the well bred horse – as you have ever done in the past."

A sobering reminder of the price paid

CHAPTER 16

MEMORIALS

Those in the forces who survived the war received medals, of which there were seven types:

- The 1914 Star. For those who came under fire during the period 5 August – 22 November 1914
- The 1914-1915 Star. For services in Flanders from 23 November 1914 – 31 December 1915, to include East and West Africa, Gallipoli and Egypt
- British War Medals 1914 – 1920
- Victory Medal
- The Mons Star. A star to pin on the 1914 medal ribbon to those who fought at Mons
- The Territorial Force Medal. For members of the Territorial Army prior to September 1914
- Mercantile Marine War Medal. To those who served in the Merchant Navy 1914 – 1918

The Victory Medal, the 1914-15 Star and the British War Medal (Author)

Servicemen who had been discharged through sickness or wounds received during the war received, in addition to the medals, a circular silver war badge inscribed with "For King and Empire, services rendered." Servicemen who had served in the British Isles did not qualify to receive any medals

After the war about 1,150,000 next of kin to those who had lost their lives, or whose death was attributable to war service up to seven years after the war ended, received a memorial plaque made from bronze gun metal with the words "He died for freedom and honour" inscribed round the edge and Britannia with her trident, a wreath and a lion in the centre. A parchment scroll with the name of the deceased read:

> "He whom this scroll commemorates was numbered among those who, at the call of King and Country, left all that was dear to them, endured hardness, faced danger, and finally passed out of sight of men by the path of duty and self-sacrifice, giving up their own lives that others may live in freedom. Let those who come after see to it that his name be not forgotten."

Accompanying the scroll was a letter from King George V which read:

> "I join with my grateful people in sending you this memorial of a brave life given for others in the Great War."

Throughout Britain between 1919 and 1922 some 37,000 war memorials were erected throughout the country with the most famous, the Cenotaph in Whitehall, being built in 1919.

Churches in the area have memorials to the dead of both the world wars. These consist of rolls of honour held within the churches or memorials situated outside. It is important to remember that these lists of the war dead do not necessarily include everyone who was a victim. Some families, still suffering private grief at the loss of a loved one, did not want their relative's name displayed on a public memorial. The lists also do not include those unfortunate soldiers who died years after the war's end through injuries

The Cenotaph, designed by Sir Edwin Lutyens, was meant to be a temporary memorial to mark Peace Day on 19 July 1919 and was made from wood and plaster, but following public demand it was rebuilt in stone in 1920 (Author)

received during the conflict; the victims of gassing in particular continued to die for years afterwards from the awful effects. Finchley Cottage Hospital, which had been opened in 1908 with 20 beds, had been requested by the War Refugee Committee to provide medical care for the many Belgian refugees in the area. Injured soldiers had also been treated there and at King Edward's Hall Auxiliary Medical Hospital in Church End, Finchley and Summerlee Auxiliary Hospital in East Finchley. After the war had ended it was decided that Finchley Cottage Hospital should be enlarged and, following a public fund raising campaign, a War Memorial extension was opened in November 1922 in memory of the men of Finchley and Whetstone who fell in the war. From then on the by now 47-bed hospital was known as Finchley Memorial.

In the memorial in the church of St James the Great in Friern Barnet Lane are the names of 87 men who were killed in the war. Every name must have a story behind it and here are a few:

THE FINCHLEY WAR MEMORIAL.

A PUBLIC MEETING

Will be held in the

Stephens Memorial Hall,

NORTH FINCHLEY,

on

THURSDAY, 7th AUGUST, 1919,

At 8 p.m.,

In Support of the Finchley War Memorial.

All Residents of Finchley are earnestly invited to attend this Meeting.

C. S. SYRETT,
Chairman of the Committee.

When you next pass 5 Glenthorne Road, Friern Barnet, remember Herbert and Ethel Broadhurst whose home it was during their brief married life. Herbert was born in 1879 in Hadley and grew up in North Finchley, youngest of the eight children of John (who was editor of *The Organist*) and Louisa Broadhurst. Herbert, following two of his brothers, became an insurance clerk. In November 1915 he enlisted in the Royal West Surrey Regiment (The Queen's). He and Edith were married in May 1916, coming to live in Friern Barnet; three months later he embarked for France. The following month he was killed in action on the Somme battlefield. Their daughter, Pauline, was born after his death. Herbert's grave is unknown; he is commemorated on the Thiepval Memorial on the Somme. Edith was awarded a pension of 18s 9d for herself and her child.

Arthur Cornell lived round the corner in Holly Park Road with his parents, Thomas (attendant at Colney Hatch Asylum) and Letitia, and his two sisters. He was baptised in St James' Church by Frederick Hall in April 1893 and was educated at St John's and Friern Lane (St James's Schools). He worked as an advertisement clerk. He enlisted very soon after the outbreak of the war in September 1914, originally in the Middlesex Regiment, later transferred to the Rifle Brigade. He, too, died in September 1916 on the Somme; he is buried in Delville Wood Cemetery on the Somme. His commanding officer wrote of him: "He was a really good man and a useful soldier." Rector Ernest Gage Hall wrote in the parish magazine; "Arthur Cornell was also among the fallen….he and his friend were killed together while lying in a shell hole."

Thomas Farrow was yet another casualty of the Somme. His parents, William, a solicitor's clerk, and Ada were Londoners, who, after their marriage in 1889, emigrated to Australia where Tom was born in 1892 and his sister, Eulalia, four years later. By 1900 the family had returned and were living in Hornsey where a second son, Alfred, was born, before moving to 6 Ramsden Road, Friern Barnet. Tom was working for a wholesale draper before the war and enlisted in the Royal Fusiliers in August 1914, immediately after the outbreak. He embarked for France in

June 1915 and in October was wounded in the head by shrapnel. After recovering, he returned to the Front, where he was killed in action in October 1916. The Rector wrote: "When last observed Tom Farrow was with a party on his way to the trenches. Shortly afterwards a shell came over and he was not seen again." Like Herbert Broadhurst he is commemorated on the Thiepval Memorial.

In April 1915 the Rector wrote:

> "Mr and Mrs Keen of the Porter's Lodge, Colney Hatch Asylum, have five sons serving Christopher and Lionel, 1st Herts. Regiment; Henry, 1st Dorset Regiment, wounded, Neville, Middlesex Regiment, stationed in Gibraltar (a few months later he was in France); and Charles, *HMS Inconstant*."

Richard Keen, an attendant (later inspector) at the Asylum, married Harriet Riches at St James's Church in 1881. They lived for many years in Glenthorne Road, where most of their six children were born, before moving to 48 Holly Park Road. All the children were baptised in St James's; Christopher Richard (born 1883), Henry James (1885), Ernest Neville (1887), Charles Montague (1889), Lionel Douglas (1892) and Edith Mary (1896). Henry and Christopher were also married at St James's, both in 1912. Henry and Charles were both in the forces before the war; Henry in the Army – he was in action with the British Expeditionary Force in Belgium within a few days of its declaration; Charles in the Royal Navy – the cruiser *HMS Inconstant* on which he served was in the Battle of Jutland. Four of his brothers survived the war; Neville (by then serving in the London Rifle Brigade and promoted to Corporal) was killed in action in France on 28 March 1918, shortly after the start of the final German offensive, which after initial success and hundreds of thousands of casualties on each side, collapsed, leading to the Armistice. He is commemorated on the Arras Memorial.

Another Friern Barnet family, the Irwins, had six sons serving in the war. Alexander and Lilian Irwin had lived in Clapham, where their first three sons were born; Alexander (1885), Ernest (1886) and Douglas (1887). They moved to Friern Barnet, living at 2 Bellevue Road, then in Hartland Road before moving to 125 Friern Barnet Road. Horace (born 1891) Sydney (1894), Irene (1895), Cyril (1898), Arthur (1900) and Kathleen (1901) were all baptised in St James's Church, where also were married Ernest (1909) and Sydney (1920). Before the war Alexander junior had emigrated to Canada; all the other sons apart from Arthur – still at school – had followed their father (who died in 1912), working as railway clerks. Alexander returned to Europe with the Canadian Scottish Regiment, Ernest served with the Leicestershire Regiment, Douglas with the Royal Garrison Artillery, Horace with the Argyll and Sutherland Highlanders, Sydney with the Machine Gun Corps and Cyril in the Royal Navy, on the destroyer *HMS Nerissa*, which took part in the Battle of Jutland. As with the Keen brothers, all but one survived. Horace, then Corporal, was awarded the Military Medal in February 1917 and commissioned as Second Lieutenant. Like Neville Keen, he died in the final year of the war, killed in action on 20 July as ground was retaken. He is buried at Marfaux British Cemetery.

John Jones was born in 1898 and attended St James's School in Friern Barnet Lane. He was regarded as exceptionally promising and stayed on after 14 years of age to be a pupil teacher. He sang in the church choir, taught in the Sunday school and by all accounts had charm and a gift for getting on with all sorts of people. He volunteered for Kitchener's Army and was killed, aged 19 and is buried somewhere in France.

A local man was posthumously awarded the Victoria Cross in 1918. Arthur Malcolm McReady-Drew was born at 8 Grove Road, New Southgate on 21 March 1888 but changed his name to Allistair Malcolm Cluny McReady-Diarmid and was educated at Queen Elizabeth's School for boys in Barnet. He joined the Middlesex Regiment (Duke of Cambridgeshire's Own) and achieved the rank of Acting Captain in the 17th (S) Batttalion. On 30 November 1917 at Moeuvres in France he led his company through a heavy German barrage and engaged the enemy, driving them back some 300 yards, inflicting many casualties and taking 27 prisoners. The next day the enemy attacked another company, killing all its officers. Allistair lead an attack and drove them back and regained the lost ground but he was killed by a bomb. He was awarded the VC on 15 March 1918 and is commemorated on the Cambrai Memorial to the Missing.

INDEX

Alexandra Palace 66, 134, 135
Allenby, General 59
Asquith, Herbert 148
AVC 48, 49
Avenue House 133

Baden Powell, Sir Robert 33
Baker, Albert William 169
Barfield, Mr 94, 95
Barnet Fair 127, 179
Barnet War Hospital 170
Barrie, James 27
Battle of the Somme, film 33
Beaverbrook, Lord 36
Belgian Refugees 62, 66, 89, 134, 135, 140
Bennett, Sydney J R 96
Beveridge, Sir William 104
Black Bull pub 174
Board of Trade 104, 140
Bolsheviks 194
Boy Scouts Association 33, 35
Brannan, George 116
British Expeditionary Force 10, 42, 48
British Summer Time 127
Broadhurst, Herbert 216
Buchan, John 27, 28
Bull & Butcher pub 114
Burke, Thomas 131
Butcher, James 19
Byng, Julian 169

Canadian Corps 169
Cavell, Edith 29, 30
Cenotaph 214
Certificate of Employment 203
Chaplin, Charlie 33

Churchill, Winston 69, 205
Clarke, Percy 49
Colman, Alfred 93
Conan Doyle, Arthur 27
Consolidation Act 1914 19
Constable, Ena 114, 190
Cook, Son & Co 46
Cooper, Charles 19
Cornell, Arthur 216
Crosby, William 200
Crouch End 191
Cuffley 176

Davidson, Ernest 160, 194
De Dion motor works 144, 204
Defence of the Realm Act (DORA) 18, 25, 132, 135
Derby, Lord 90
Despard, Charlotte 138
Dove, Ellen 170
Dukes, E J, Rev 136
Dymoke, Albert E 94

East Barnet War Memorial 169
Edmonton Council 116
Eligibility of Women Act 150
Elliot, W 44
Entente Cordiale 7
Ewen Hall 133

Farrow, Thomas 217
Finchley Board School 22
Finchley Memorial Hospital 214, 215
Finchley Voluntary Nurses' Fund 200
Flack, H J 19
Food Hoarding Order 114
Food Vigilance Committee 113
Forces' Post Office 56, 62
Franz Ferdinand, Archduke 8

Franz Ferdinand, Emperor 6
French, General 76
Friary Park Bowling Club 129
Friern Barnet Court 94
Friern Barnet Grammar School 84
Friern Barnet Relief Fund 22

Gage Hall, E, Rev 136
Gates, Horace 94
Gear, Gillian 114
George V, King 10, 135, 213
Giant bomber 188
Glenart Castle, HMS 145
Goschen, Sir Edward 9
Gotha bomber 188
Gray, Anthea 58
Gray, William Lionel 58, 59, 81, 82
Grey, Sir Edward 9, 11
Grovelands House 133

Haig, Sir Douglas 210
Hall & Co 200
Hardie, Keir 137
Harrison, Rose 158
Hardy, Thomas 27
Hart, Charles 93
Henry, Charlotte 145
Hitler, Adolf 207
Holden, Henry 200
Hollybrook Memorial 145
Holly Park School 116, 175
Holman, Gerald 76, 78
Holman, Mabel 21, 59, 117, 146, 180, 191, 198
Horton, Charles Thomas 40

Imperial Service 160
Ivernia, HMS 40
Irwin family 218

Johnson, Jack 39, 40
Jones, John 218

Keen, Neville 218
Keen, Richard 217
King Edward's Hall Hospital 214
Kipling, Rudyard 27
Kirkham Jones, T 43
Kitchener, Lord 13, 14, 69, 90, 135, 138

Land Cultivation Order 116
Laurie, William 200
Law, Bonar 207
Lawrence, Dorothy 145
Lawrence, T E 58, 59
League of Nations 206
Linsey, Mrs 40
Liquor Control Regulations 135
Lloyd George, David 17, 28, 33, 75, 99, 135, 208
LGOC 142
London Electrical Engineers 160
London Rifle Brigade 217
London Underground 141, 175
Lusitania, RMS 20, 21
Lutyens, Sir Edwin 214

Maison Lyons 129, 130
Manor Farm Dairies 170
Mathey, Heinrich 175
McCrae, John 208
McCready-Diarmid, Allister 218
McCurd Lorry Factory 144, 145
Mercantile Marine war medal 212
Middlesex Prisoners of War Fund 200
Middlesex Regiment 23, 68, 167, 169
Middlesex Volunteer Regiment 84
Military Cross 168
Military Service Act 92, 93

Mill Hill Barracks 167, 170
Ministry of Food 110
Mons Star 212
Muswell Hill 58, 71, 117, 180
Muswell Hill Station 74

Nash, Fraser 172
Nicholas II, Tsar 6, 193
North Middlesex Golf Club 23, 129

Oakdene Nursing Home 172
Orange Tree pub 195

Palmers Green 175
Pankhurst, Adele 148
Pankhurst, Christabel 148
Pankhurst, Emmeline 148
Pankhurst, Sylvia 148
Parr, John 22, 23
Patch, Harry 205
Post Office 140, 141
Potters Bar 177, 180, 181
Princip, Gavrilo 8
Priors department store 200
Public Meals Order 108

Rasputin 6
Reboul, Percy 160, 173
Red Cross 89, 200
Representation of the People Act 150
Ridden, Rifleman W 41
Robinson, Leefe 175, 176
Royal Engineers 161
Royal Flying Corps 47, 173, 187
Royal Navy 108
Royal Horticultural Society 116
RSPCA 49

Russell, Bertrand 138
Rusted, Lance Sergeant 90

Sanders, William 93
Sassoon, Siegfried 138, 173
Saunders, H A 145
Schlieffen Plan 7, 9
Scots Greys 67
Shoulder Arms, film 33
Smale, Wilfred 168
Smith, Hubert A 94
Southgate Urban District Council 134
Spanish flu 191
Special constables 179, 182, 184
St James Church 145
St James School 119
Stroud Green Station 70
Suffragettes 147, 148
Summerlee Auxiliary Hospital 214

Tempest, Wulstan 175, 177
Territorial Army 160
Territorial Force Medal 212
Tilley, A C 38
Tilley, Geoffrey 42
Tottenham Hotspur 165
Treaty of Versailles 206
Tull, Walter 165, 166, 167, 168
Turner, Sidney 93

Vacant Land Cultivation Society 116
VADs 132, 133, 179
Vardon, Henry 190
Victoria Cross 218
Victory medal 212
von Bismarck, Otto 6

WAACs 143
War Bonds 101, 103
War Office 126
War Savings Certificates 100, 101
Waterloo, Battle of 12
Webb, Beatrice 173
Weir, James 200
Wells, H G 27
Westminster Dragoons 60
Wilhelm II, Kaiser 10, 12, 21, 194
Wilson, Woodrow 192
Women's Forestry Corps 143
Women's Institute 144
Women's Land Army 143
Women's Social and Political Union 148
Woodhouse School 168
Woodward, Vivian 165
WRNS 143
Wrotham Park 169

Zimmerman, Arthur 192

APPENDIX A
CHRONOLOGY
THE HOME FRONT

1914

4 Aug	Britain declares war on Germany. The Railway Executive Committee immediately takes overall charge of Britain's railways
5 Aug	Lord Kitchener becomes Secretary of State for War
8 Aug	Defence of the Realm Act is passed
12 Aug	Britain declares war on Austria-Hungary
17 Aug	Enrolment of Special Constables commences
28 Aug	Appeal for an extra 100,000 men for the Army
11 Sep	Blackout in London
18 Sep	Trading with the Enemy Act imposes severe penalties on anyone trading with Germany
28 Sep	Prince Louis of Battenburg resigns as First Sea Lord
29 Sep	Lord Fisher appointed First Sea Lord
16 Oct	First Canadian troops arrive in England
24 Oct	Import of sugar is banned
5 Nov	Britain declares war on Turkey and annexes Cyprus

17 Nov	War Loan of £350 million is issued
	Lloyd George presents first war Budget

1915

1 Jan	Military Cross is introduced
4 Feb	Germany declares the waters around Britain a war region
8 Mar	Bill introduced to give Government control of munitions production
17 Mar	War Service Register for Women is introduced
5 Apr	King George prohibits use of alcoholic drinks in any royal household
22 Apr	Passenger traffic between England and Holland suspended
4 May	Budget estimates a revenue of £270 million
7 May	*RMS Lusitania* is sunk. Anti-German riots follow
16 Jun	Lloyd George is appointed Minister of Munitions
23 Jun	Carl Frederick Muller shot as German spy in Tower of London
24 Jun	Coalition Government is formed under Prime Minister Herbert Asquith
29 Jun	National Registration Act for everyone between 15 and 65
2 Jul	Ministry of Munitions is formed
13 Jul	Strikes are outlawed

15 Jul	Welsh miners strike until 20 July
30 Jul	Haicke Janssen and Willem Roos shot as spies in Tower of London
15 Aug	National Registration for 15-25 olds
25 Aug	Welsh miners refuse to sign no-strike agreement
9 Sep	Ernst Melin shot as a German spy in Tower of London
17 Sep	Augusto Roggen shot as a German spy in Tower of London
19 Sep	Fernando Buschmann shot as a German spy in Tower of London
21 Sep	Budget introduces new taxes
27 Sep	600 Austrians and Germans interned in Alexandra Palace
15 Oct	Britain declares war on Bulgaria
26 Oct	George Breeckow shot as German spy in Tower of London
27 Oct	Irving Reis shot as German spy in Tower of London
2 Dec	Albert Meyer shot as a spy in Tower of London

1916

9 Feb	Military Service Act introduces conscription for men between 18 and 41
23 Feb	Lord Robert Cecil is appointed Minister of Blockade
6 Mar	Women's National Land Service is started
18 Mar	Royal Defence Corps is formed

4 Apr	Budget introduces taxes on amusements, matches and mineral waters and increase in income tax
11 Apr	Ludovico Zender shot as a German spy in Tower of London
24 Apr	Outbreak of Irish rebellion
25 Apr	Sinn Fein sympathisers seize Dublin Post Office
26 Apr	Martial Law in Dublin declared
28 Apr	Martial Law introduced across whole of Ireland
30 Apr	Dublin Post Office burned by Irish nationalists
3 May	Military Service Bill is extended to married men
	Three Irish leaders shot
5 May	Four Irish rebels shot
8 May	Four more Irish rebels shot
11 May	Twelve Irish rebels shot, 73 more sentenced to penal servitude and 6 to life imprisonment
15 May	Sir Roger Casement charged with high treason
21 May	Daylight Saving Bill comes into force
6 June	Lord Kitchener is drowned as *HMS Hampshire* is sunk by a mine
29 Jun	Sir Roger Casement found guilty of treason and sentenced to death
6 Jul	David Lloyd George becomes Secretary of State for War
9 Jul	E S Montagu appointed Minister of Munitions

13 Jul	Bank Holiday is suspended
22 Jul	A silver badge is introduced for those disabled while serving in the forces
21 Aug	The film, *Battle of the Somme*, is released
14 Nov	Pensions Bill introduced
17 Nov	Food regulations introduced
20 Nov	Board of Trade introduces regulations on milk and flour
29 Nov	Boart of Trade takes over South Wales coalfields
5 Dec	Lloyd George and Herbert Asquith resign
7 Dec	Lloyd George becomes Prime Minister
9 Dec	New War Cabinet is formed. Ministries of Food, Labour and Shipping are formed
11 Dec	Ministry of Labour is formed

1917

19 Jan	Large explosion at Silvertown, 73 killed, 400 injured and 60,000 properties damaged
31 Jan	Germany declares unrestricted naval warfare on all neutral states
15 Feb	Government takes over all coal mines in Britain
16 Mar	Potato famine in England
19 Mar	The 8 hour day is made legal

20 Mar	Ministry of National Service is formed
28 Mar	Women's Army Auxiliary Corps is formed
3 Apr	A strike of Barrow shipyard workers is ended
6 Apr	A Food Hoarding Order is introduced
18 Apr	A Food Order restricts the making of pastries and cakes
30 Apr	The Jockey Club decides to stop racing after 4 May
14 May	London bus workers strike
16 May	Lloyd George proposes Home Rule for Ireland
15 Jun	Lord Rhondda appointed Food Controller
21 Jun	Order of the British Empire is formed
25 Jun	First American troops arrive in England
17 Jul	Change of name to House of Windsor
	Winston Churchill appointed Minister of Munitions
21 Aug	Ministry of Reconstruction formed
8 Sep	Price of milk set at 8d per quart for 3 months
18 Sep	Sir A Yapp is made Food Controller
21 Nov	Conscientious Objectors are disenfranchised
29 Nov	Women's Royal Naval Service is formed

1918

10 Feb	Lord Beaverbrook appointed Minister in charge of Propaganda
25 Feb	Meat, butter and margarine are rationed in London and Home Counties
28 Mar	Women's Auxiliary Army Corps is formed
1 Apr	Royal Air Force is formed
7 Apr	Meat rationing introduced across Britain
22 Jun	Home Rule proposals and conscription in Ireland are abandoned
9 Jul	J R Clynes appointed Food Controller
23 Jul	Munitions workers go on strike in Coventry
24 Jul	Munitions workers go on strike in Birmingham
29 Jul	Munitions workers return to work
31 Jul	Sir Charles Fielding appointed Director General of Food Production
30 Aug	London police go on strike for a day
30 Oct	Influenza epidemic – 2,200 deaths in a week in London
7 Nov	Civil Department of Demobilisation and Resettlement is formed
11 Nov	Armistice is declared

APPENDIX B
CHRONOLOGY
THE WESTERN FRONT

1914

6 Aug	Austria-Hungary declares war on Russia. Serbia declares war on Germany
7 Aug	British Expeditionary Force (BEF) lands in France
12 Aug	Britain declares war on Austria-Hungary
20 Aug	German troops occupy Brussels
23 Aug	BEF retreats from Mons
26 Aug	Battle of Le Cateau. BEF retreats
3 Sep	*HMS Pathfinder* sunk by U-boat
5 Sep	Germans capture Rheims
6 Sep	Battle of the Marne begins
12 Sep	Germany takes Ghent and Lille
14 Sep	First Battle of Aisne
22 Sep	British cruisers *Aboukir, Cresy* & *Hogue* sunk in North Sea
24 Sep	Battle of Aisne reaches stalemate
25 Sep	First Battle of Albert
28 Sep	End of Battle of Aisne

29 Sep	Turkey joins the war in support of Germany. Germans lose Battle of Albert
7 Oct	Germans bombard Antwerp
11 Oct	Germans bomb Paris. Battle of Flanders begins
14 Oct	Belgian government flees to France
19 Oct	Battle of Ypres begins
20 Oct	*Glitra* is first merchant ship to be sunk by a U-boat.
31 Oct	Turkey attacks Russian fleet.
20 Nov	Bulgaria declares neutrality. First Battle of Champagne
22 Nov	First Battle of Ypres ends
27 Nov	Russians rout Germans in Poland
3 Dec	Belgium is under control of German army

1915

31 Jan	Tear gas used for first time, against Russians
11 Feb	First Canadian soldiers land in France
12 Feb	French begin offensive at Champagne
18 Feb	German blockade of Britain begins
10 Mar	British take Neuve Chapelle
20 Mar	French offensive in Champagne fails
20 Apr	President Wilson declares USA neutral

22 Apr	Second battle of Ypres begins. First German gas attacks
25 Apr	Allied forces land in Dardanelles
26 Apr	Allied forces land at Gallipoli
30 Apr	Germany invades Baltic Provinces
22 May	Germans bomb Paris
13 Jul	New German offensive at Argonne
25 Jul	First RFC fighter squadron (No 11) arrives in France
30 Jul	Germans use flame throwers at Hooge.
24 Aug	Start of 13 day continuous artillery duel on Western Front
25 Aug	French and British offensives in Artois and Champagne end in stalemate
31 Aug	Germany and Austria-Hungary partition Poland
22 Sep	Second Battle of Champagne begins
25 Sep	Battle of Loos begins
26 Sep	Allied offensive in Flanders
29 Sep	French capture Vimy Ridge
11 Oct	Edith Cavell executed in Brussels
15 Oct	Britain declares war on Bulgaria
16 Oct	France declares war on Bulgaria
15 Dec	Sir John French is replaced as Head of British Forces by Sir Douglas Haig

18 Dec	Battle of Verdun ends
20 Dec	Gallipoli campaign abandoned by Allies

1916

8 Jan	Allied forces evacuated from Gallipoli
7 Feb	RFC forms first single-seat fighter squadron (No 24)
21 Feb	Battle of Verdun begins
2 Jun	Third Battle of Ypres starts
24 Jun	Week-long Britih artillery bombardment on Somme
1 Jul	Battle of the Somme at Picardy begins
3 Jul	First RFC aircraft with synchronised propeller/gun mechanism with 70 suadron
15 Jul	British win Battle of Delville Wood
3 Sep	Start of Battle of Guillemont
15 Sep	Tanks used for first time, on the Somme
25 Sep	Battles of Morval and Thiepval Ridge lead to Allied advance
1 Oct	Battle of Ancre Heights until 11 October. Battle of Transloy Ridges until 20 October
13 Nov	Battle of Ancre starts fourth phase of Battle of Somme
18 Nov	Battle of the Somme ends
15 Dec	French launch massive assault on Verdun

18 Dec	Battle of Verdun ends.

1917

16 Jan	Zimmerman telegram
22 Jan	US President Wilson calls for "peace without victory"
1 Feb	Germany declares unrestricted submarine warfare
3 Feb	USA severs diplomatic relations with Germany
9 Feb	German retreat 25 miles to Hindenburg Line
23 Feb	RFC No 100 squadron, first night bomber squadron, arrives in France
12 Mar	Start of Russian Revolution
15 Mar	Tsar Nicholas abdicates
6 Apr	USA declares war on Germany
9 Apr	Battle of Arras begins
16 Apr	Second Battle of the Aisne
17 Apr	French tanks used for the first time
20 Apr	Third Battle of the Somme.
29 Apr	Mutiny in the French Army
3 May	British break through Hindenburg Line east of Arras
16 May	British capture Bullecourt in Battle of Arras
7 Jun	British forces capture Messines Ridge and explode mines

31 Jul	Third Battle of Ypres (Passchendaele) begins
20 Aug	Third Battle of Verdun starts
28 Aug	French recapture all ground lost since 1916
9 Oct	Third phase of Battle of Ypres
12 Oct	British offensive at Passchendaele
27 Oct	US troops in action in France for the first time
6 Nov	Passchedaele village captured by Canadians
11 Nov	Third Battle of Ypres ends
20 Nov	Battle of Cambrai begins – first use of massed tanks
25 Nov	German counter attack at Cambrai and regain lost ground
29 Nov	Russian and German armistice
4 Dec	Battle of Cambrai ends

1918

21 Mar	German Spring Offensive starts along 50 mile front
22 Mar	Germans take 16,000 prisoners as they reach the Somme
23 Mar	Germans shell Paris with Big Bertha, 43 ton howitzer
28 Mar	Germany sustains heavy losses in River Scarpe area
21 Apr	Baron Manfred von Richtofen, "The Red Baron" is killed
29 Apr	British inflict heavy losses on 13 German Infantry Divisions
27 May	Third Battle of Aisne

4 Jun	US troops check German advance at Veuilluy Wood
6 Jun	Germans suffer huge losses at Bellau Wood
9 Jun	Start of First Battle of Lassigny, and Battle of Noyon
15 Jul	Second Battle of the Marne
16 Jul	Tsar Nicholas and family murdered
19 Jul	Germans retreat at the Marne
4 Aug	Second Battle of the Marne ends
8 Aug	Allied counter-offensive launched at Amiens, Germans defeated
9 Aug	Second Battle of Lassigny
12 Aug	End of Battle of Amiens – heavy defeat of Germans
14 Aug	Germans retreat from River Ancre
17 Aug	French push Germans off Aisne
29 Aug	French capture Noyon, British capture Bapaume
1 Sep	British capture Peronne. French advance north of Noyon
2 Sep	British capture Cagnicourt, Villers and Queant
4 Sep	Germans retreat to Hindenburg line
18 Sep	British attack outposts of Hindenburg line
26 Sep	Hindenberg Line is broken
27 Sep	Second Battle of Cambrai
28 Sep	Bulgaria surrenders. Battle of Flanders

1 Oct	Ludendorff says Germany must request immediate ceasefire
4 Oct	Germans send request to President Wilson for armistice
5 Oct	End of Second Battle of Cambrai
8 Oct	President Wilson demands Germany withdraws from occupied territories
9 Oct	Cambrai taken by British
10 Oct	British take Le Cateau. Germans retreat from Argonne Forest
12 Oct	End of Second Battle of Le Cateau and Battle for Champagne
17 Oct	Belgians retake Ostend, British liberate Lille and enter Dou
22 Oct	British enter Valenciennes
23 Oct	President Wilson refuses to deal with existing German government. German line pushed back three miles
25 Oct	Battle of the Selle ends
29 Oct	Mutiny in German army
31 Oct	Germany appeals for armistice
1 Nov	British reach Valenciennes
3 Nov	Austria surrenders. German fleet mutinies at Kiel. Belgians advance to Ghent
4 Nov	Anglo-French offensive along 30 mile front. Last major attack of the war
8 Nov	Uprisings in Munich and ten other German cities

10 Nov   Kaiser Wilhelm flees to Holland

11 Nov   Armistice signed at 5.00 am. Cease fire takes place at 11.00am

APPENDIX C
THE WAR DEAD

The following names are recorded in churches and other memorials in Finchley, Friern Barnet and Whetstone. Biographical details have been sourced from Forces War Records (www.forces-war-records.co.uk).

Details of names in churches in High Barnet, East Barnet and New Barnet are being recorded by Barnet & District Local History Society.

ALL SAINTS' CHURCH, Oakleigh Road North, Whetstone

Abrahams, Ernest   *Corporal, Royal Engineers. Died 5 June 1915. Helles Memorial, Gallipoli*

Barlow, Frederick

Beels, Albert   *Corporal, Cameron Highlanders. Died 2 September 1918 age 20. Son of Alfred Beels, 6 Lily Villas, Whetstone*

Bothwell, Duncan   *Sapper, Royal Engineers. Died 19 October 1918 age 31. Etaples Military Cemetery. Husband of Mrs Bothwell, 2 Derwent Villas, High Road, Whetstone*

Brown, Henry

Brown, Walter

Barfield, Claude   *Lieutenant, Royal Flying Corps. Died 29 June 1915 age 29. Hazebrouk Comm. Cemetery. Son of Cllr. John Barfield, Thatcham, Whetstone High Road. "Engine failed on take off"*

Christie, George   *Private, Middlesex Regiment. Died 1 October 1915. Helles memorial. Son of Henry Christie, North Villa, Athenaeum Road, Whetstone*

Christie, Sydney *Sergeant, DCLI. Died 16 July 1916 age 21. "Attack on High Wood. War diary records troops muddy and disreputable but all quite happy and tired out."*

Claridge, Alfred *Possibly Rifleman KRRC. Died 8 July 1916 age 17. Carnoy Military Cemetery, son of Harry Claridge, 4 Oakleigh Road North, Whetstone. "At Poperinghe, worked on bridging and road repair, High casualties while working"*

Clarke, Edgar *Either Henry Clarke of 7 Ivy Villas or Herbert Clarke of 34 Pollard Road, Whetstone*

Coe, Ernest *Private, Middlesex Regiment. Died 6 November 1918 age 20. Cross Roads Cemetery, Fontaine aux Bois. Son of Ernest Coe, 46 Pollard Road, Whetstone*

Cox, Leslie *Rifleman, KRRC. Died 5 May 1915. Ypres Menin Gate. Husband of Mrs Cox, 10 Oakview Terrace, Oakleigh Road, Whetstone*

Cox, Norman F *Acting Sergeant, Bedfordshire Regiment. Died 29 April 1917 age 24. Arras Memorial. Husband of Mrs Cox, 10 Oakview Terrace, Whetstone*

Cranston, John F *Private, Middlesex Regiment. Died 26 August 1918 age 34. Vermelles BNr Cemetery. Slaughterman, single. Son of Mrs Cranston, 5 Bass Cottages, Whetstone*

Edwards, William *Husband of Mrs Edwards, 10 Russell Road, Whetstone*

Frampton, Stanley *Private, Bedfordshire Regiment. Died of wounds 3 November 1918. Cannock Chase War Cemetery. Son of E Frampton, 48 Russell Road, Whetstone*

Grimsey, Harry *Private, Middlesex Regiment. Died 3 September 1916. Thirepval Memorial. "Attack on Thiepval Chateau. During this attack Pts. F Edward and R Ryder awarded Victoria Crosses. Practically every yard was contested."*

Grimsey, Joseph *Private, Middlesex Regiment. Died 24 November 1917. Cambrai Memorial, Louvernal. Husband of Mrs Grimsey, 3 Doncaster Terrace, Whetstone*

Grimsey, Thomas *Private, London Regiment. Died 4 October 1917. Tyne Cott memorial. Husband of Mrs E Grimsey, 5 Doncaster Terrace, Whetstone*

Hinds, George *Rifleman, KRRC. Died 15 April 1918. Ploegstreet Memorial. Son of William Hinds, 13 Cecil Cottages, Rasper Road, Whetstone*

Hudson, W J *Gunner, RFA. Died 1 March 1918. Oxford Cenetery. Son of W J Hudson, Athenaeum Road, Whetstone*

Hunt, H W *Fitter Cpl, Royal Engineers. Died 5 November 1916. Thiepval Memorial. Son of Harry Hunt, 42 Russell Road, Whetstone*

Hunt, J H *Private, Middlesex Hussars. Died 18 October 1918. Alexandra (Hadra) War Memorial Cemetery. Son of John Hunt, Deodora Grange, Oakleigh Road, Whetstone*

Jones, Allen

Levy, Joseph *Private, London Regiment. Died 10 December 1917. St Vaast Military Cemetery. Son of Jospeh Levy, 1 Guy Cliffe Cottages, High Road, Whetstone*

Lindsay, Albert *Possibly Private, RASC. Died of wounds 18 February 1919 age 28. Mombasa British Memorial. Possibly son of A Lindsay, Haldon, Friern Barnet Lane*

McDonald, Douglas

Moore, C *Husband of Mrs Moore, Woodlands, Oakleigh Park South, Whetstone*

Morley, William *Possibly son of Samuel Morley, fishmonger, High Road, Whetstone or Thomas Moore, Cattle Dealer, Russells Farm, Whetstone*

Oakley, Frank *Son of Henry Oakley, The Laurels, High Road, Whetstone*

Ovens, Henry *Corporal, Middlesex Regiment. Died 8 October 1916. Thiepval Memorial. "Hand to hand fighting while securing Zenith Trench. Casualties 243."*

Palmer, W   *Son of Albert Palmer, 6 Sunnyside, Swan Lane, Whetstone or Henry Palmer, 37 Birley Road, Whetstone*

Parfitt, David   *Private, RWF. Died 28 February 1918. Mervill Com Extn Cemetery. Son of Fred Pargitt, 15 Bawtry Road, Whetstone*

Proctor, Alfred   *Possibly Private, Middlesex Regiment. Died 18 May 1917. Duissans Cemetery, Etrun, son of Alfred Proctor, Lime Cottage, High Road, Whetstone*

Scott, Thomas   *Son of Alexander Scott, 134 Balfour Grove, Whetstone*

Smith, Walter

Spreat, L H   *Second Lieutenant, RFA. Died 8 October 1916 age 19. Grove Town Cemetery, Meaulte. "Failed to return."*

Stokoe, John   *Private, Northumberland Fusiliers. Died 26 September 1915. Adanac Military Cemetery, Miramaunt*

Thompson, Ernest   *Possibly son of George Thompson, 43 Russell Road, Whetstone*

Turner, Arthur

Waters, Arthur

Waters, Harry

COLNEY HATCH LUNATIC ASYLUM

Baker, George (attendant)   *Private, 4th Battalion Royal Fusiliers. Missing in France December 1914*

Clark, Arthur (boiler stoker)   *Lance Corporal, 1st Battalion Grenadier Guards. Died in France 2 November 1918*

Dickens, Charles Albert (attendant) *Private, 4th Battalion, Royal Fusiliers. Missing in France December 1914*

Henderson, William Richard (attendant) *Trooper, First Royal Dragoons Missing in France 30 October 1914*

Humphreys, Maxwell Mark (attendant) *Lance Corporal, South Wales Borderers. Missing in France 18 December 1914*

Lamont, John (House Steward's 1st Clerk) *Private, 4th Battalion County of London Regiment (London Scottish). Killed in Arras 12 March 1918*

Reynolds, John (gas stoker) *Sapper, 22nd Field Company Royal Engineers. Died in France 15 July 1918*

FINCHLEY COUNTY SCHOOL, Solomon's Court, 451 High Road, N12

Memorial Plaque: LIVE THOU FOR ENGLAND: WE FOR ENGLAND DIED

Allsopp, W *Private, Middlesex Regiment. Killed 1 July 1916 age 24. Husband of Jessie Allsopp 158 Coltenham Road, Upper Holloway*

Boyce, G

Burton, C R

Carter, H W

Chennell, L F H

Chennell, R

Collins, G G

Dutton, H

Garrard, E

Hadland, F *Private, Gloucestershire Regiment. Killed 23 August 1918 age 19. Parents George Thomas and F M Hadland, 21 Queens Road, Finchley*

Halsey, A

Hayward, H R

Hearne, L

Lovegrove, A S

McBeath, W M

Newham, F *Rifleman, London Regiment. Died of wounds 15 October 1916*

Oulet, J *Private Queen's (Royal West Surrey Regiment). Died 9 July 1916 age 21. Son of Mr and Mrs J I Oulet, "Ava" 188 Nether Street, Finchley*

Ovens, H *Corporal, Middlesex Regiment. Killed 8 October 1916*

Pointing, L *Lance Corporal, Honourable Artillery. Died 15 November 1916 age 26. Son of James and Mary Ann Pointing, 22 Churchfield Avenue, North Finchley*

Rogers, A

Rogers, F

Shaw, W

Stevens, D

Taylor, W D

Thornett, C *Sergeant, London Regiment. Killed 18 August 1918 age 23*

Warren, R G

Weir, J *Lance Corporal, Middlesex Regiment. Killed 16 October 1918*

Welch, R *Private London Regiment. Killed 15 November 1916 age 22. Parents Amos Edwin and Annie Welch, 4 Woodside Cottages, Whetstone*

West, A W

METROPOLITAN ELECTRIC TRAMWAYS FINCHLEY DEPOT
(Plaque outside 307, Ballards Lane, N12)

Boardman, J L

Bowen, J E

Clark, H

Edwards, R H

Emery, J *Possibly Private, Middlesex Regiment. Died 25 October 1918*

Field, E H

Griffin, W

Hampson, C O

Kirk, T

Mitchell, A

Moore, W T

Onslow, A W

Peddell, T W

Redfearn, J *Sergeant, Middlesex Regiment. Died 28 May 1917 age 35. Husband of Maude Emily Redfearn of 23 Avenue Road, North Finchley*

Robins, R

Sharpe, J

Swift, E A

Tinsley, R

NORTH MIDDLESEX GOLF CLUB Memorial plaque in grounds

Baker, James H   *Second Lieutenant, 8th Yorks and Lancs. Died 1 July 1916. Parents James Henry and Charlotte Isabella Baker of Friern Lodge, Friern Lane, Whetstone*

Edwards, Roy   *Lieutenant, 10th Rifle Brigade*

Gilpatrick Given, B A, G   *Colonial Government Services*

Hetherington, J E   *Lieutenant, 1st Canadian Motor Machine Gun Brigade*

Isaac, William James   *Second Lieutenant, 2nd 10th London Regiment. Died 26 April 1916*

Kynoch, Alex Bruce   *Captain, West Riding Regiment & RFC*

Melhuish, Frank   *Rifleman, London Rifle Brigade. Died 9 October 1916*

Pope-Bennett, W H   *Captain, 13th Royal Sussex*

Wilding, Godfrey J   *Lieutenant, The Kings Own Royal Lancaster*

Windsor, W J   *RNVR*

ST JAMES THE GREAT CHURCHYARD, Friern Barnet Lane

Brown, Harry   *Private, PWO Civil Service Rifles. Died 24 February 1915 age 21*

Champ, Lionel Bertram   *Sapper, Royal Engineers. Died 8 March 1919 age 33.*

Coleman, Alfred W   *Private, East Kent Regiment (The Buffs). Died 11 September 1916*

Cooper, G A   *Gunner, Royal Field Artillery. Died 27 August 1919*

Evans, Percy Llewellyn   *Sergeant, Middlesex Regiment. Died 12 February 1917 age 30*

Ferguson, Monica   *Died at Military Hospital Colchester 21 November 1918*

Hodgson, P E   *Gunner, Royal Field Artillery. Died 21 August 1918 age 40*

ST JAMES THE GREAT CHURCH, Friern Barnet Lane

In addition to the First World War memorial in the churchyard of St James The Great, there are other memorials to individuals within the churches of St James the Great and St John the Evangelist, Friern Barnet Road. There are also family graves where a war casualty, although buried elsewhere, is commemorated in the inscription. The First World War Memorial is in the shape of a cross, the work of Martin Travers of Fulham. Names were invited of all soldiers, sailors, airmen or nurses who died on active service and who were living at the time of their enlistment in the Ecclesiastical Parish of St James and St John, Friern Barnet or who were habitual worshippers at either of these churches, not restricted to Church members. The memorial was dedicated in 1921 by the Rector of Friern Barnet, the Revd Edward Gage Hall. It bears the inscription:

1914-1919

Brothers who died for our homes and country,

we salute you, and commend you to the Redeemer's keeping

Eighty seven names follow, and, beneath them, the quotation:

> "Whose glory was redressing human wrong"

The inscription is now almost completely illegible. The following list is reproduced from a report of the dedication in *Barnet Press* of 4 June 1921:

Baggs, Henry E	Field, Herbert T	Philpott, Edward C
Baker, George	Green, Alexander G	Presser, John
Beavis, Thomas	Guy, William F	Price, Alfred L
Bell, Leo	Hardie, Bernard	Price, Walter H
Bigwood, Frank	Harrison, Ronald	Reynolds, John
Bennett, W H P	Harding, E Frank	Rawlings, Percy G
Bennett, Percy D	Henderson, William R	Pitt, Robert T
Briggs, P Douglas	Henry, Charlotte E	Ridley, Alfred E
Broadhurst, Herbert H	Howitt, William	Rumbold, William P
Buttifant, Frank W	Haselwood, R T G	Sexton, Leonard A
Bussell, Travis P	Hunt, Jack H	Sims, Arthur E
Clark, Arthur	Hunt, Harry W	Sherrington, Frank T
Collins, Ronald E	Hughes, Ernest E	Sherrington, Ralph H
Cornell, Arthur J H	Hewlett, Lawrence H	Sinclair, Clifford H
Cottam, James M	Hucklesby, J	Standley, Ernest G
Cox, George O	Hucklesby, Sidney	Thorpe, George N

Cox, Thomas	Humphreys, M M	Tingley, John
Cox, Wilfred H G	Irwin, Horace C	Toms, Cecil W
Coleman. Alfred W*	Keen, Neville E	Toms, Philip R
Curry, Edgar	Kiteley, George H	Turner, Harold E
Crumpler, Arthur J	Kynoch, Alexander B	Turner, Sydney R
Davies, Alfred	List, Ronald H	Usher, Ernest E
Davies, Ivor T	Lamont, John	Vears, Ernest E
Dee, Reginald	Mackie, James	Vears, Hector W
Dickens, Charles A	Mecoy, James A	Wall, Oliver C
Fone, Stanley J	Mildern, Atholl	Wilkinson, William
Farrow, Thomas W	Mildern, Athollh	Wilmott, Albert M
Ferguson, Monica M *	Mildern, Jospeh	Wright-Ingle, Cecil
Foreman, Harold M	Paul, William	Wright, William

* Duplicate of name on gravestone in churchyard

ST JOHN THE APOSTLE, High Road, Whetstone

Adams, George *Private, 17 Battalion, Middlesex Regiment. Died 28 July 1916. Battle of Somme Thiepval Memorial cemetery. War diary says"Strong German counter attack repulsed" Son of William Adams, 37 Chandos Avenue, Whetstone*

Ayres, Frederick *Probably Private, London Rifle Brigade Died 9 October 1916 age 21. Thiepval. "Attacked and captured Switch trench"*

Bartlett, George *Private, Middlesex Regiment. Died 13 April 1917 age 23. Walincourt Cemetery, Saulty. Son of Oliver Bartlett, Littlewood, Oakleigh Road, Whetstone*

Batt, A *Private, Inniskilling Fusiliers. Died 21 November 1917. Gouzeacourt Military Cemetery. Son of Alfred Batt, 4 Southview Terrace, Fredericks Place, Whetstone*

Berkeley, T *Possibly Lieutenant, Suffolk Regiment. Died 9 November 1918 age 32. Tezze British Cemetery, Italy*

Bothwell, Duncan *Sapper, Royal Engineers. Died of wounds 19 October 1918 age 31. Etaples Military Cemetery. Husband of Mrs Bothwell, 2 Derwent Villas, Whetstone*

Bowen, J

Brown, H

Brown, W

Brice, R *Private, Middlesex Regiment. Died 12 October 1918 age 25. Romeries Com Cemetery. Son of Thomas Brice, Camelot, High Road, Whetstone*

Camfferman, A *Corporal, Middlesex Regiment. Died 9 May 1915. age 20. Fleurbaix Military Cemetery. Son of John Camfferman, nurseryman, 19 Sunnyside, Swan Lane, Whetstone. "Attack on Aubers Ridge. Casualties 82"*

Christmas, A *Lance Corporal, Middlesex Regiment. Died 19 May 1916 age 30. Doullens Extn Cemetery*

Clack, C *Private, Bedfordshire Regiment. Died 13 November 1916. Ancre British Cemetery, Beaumont Hamel. "Took part in attacks on Frankfort & Munich trenches. Heavy casualties"*

Clark, R

Clark, W E *Sapper, Royal Engineers. Died 24 March 1918 age 34. Noyon Military Cemetery*

Cook, J

Cook, T

Copping, John   *Sergeant, RASC. Died of wounds 18 February 1919 age 28. Terrlingham Cemetery, Wimille*

Dennis, F   *Possibly Corporal Rifle Brigade. Died 29 March 1917 age 24. Gouzeaucourt Military Cemetery. Son of Albert Dennis, & Friern Place, Oakleigh Road, Whetstone*

Fitz, H   *Private, Royal Irish Regiment. Died 5 April 1917 age 34. Kemmel Chateau Cemetery. Brother of William Fitz, 4 Cecil Cottages, Rasper Road, Whetstone*

Foster, J

Gentle, John   *Private, Royal Marines Light Infantry. Died 25 January 1917 age 22. Chatham Naval Memorial. Son of Thomas Gentle, 33 Oakleigh Road, Whetstone*

Goody, Geoffrey   *Lieutenant, KRRC. Died 14 July 1918 age 28. Terlingham Military Cemetery, Wimille*

Goody, Gilbert Alexander   *Acting Second Lieutena,, KRRC. Died 6 November 1916 age 28. Grove Town Military Cemetery, Meaulte*

Hall, H

Hoare, A   *Private, Middlesex Regiment. Died 15 September 1916. Thiepval Memorial. Son of Henry Hoare, 14 Sherwood Street, Whetstone. "In action at Boulaix Wood. A& C Companies moved forward at 8.20am. In a moment they were practically annihilated leaving just 25 men. Colonel King records 300 out of 500 killed"*

Howard, G

Howes, Charles   *Private, London Regiment. Died 201 October 1918 age 25. Hamburg Cemetery*

Hulbert, Thomas *Private, Royal West Kent. Died 20 April 1918 age 20. Son of Thomas Hulbert, 27 Sunnyside, Swan Lane, Whetstone*

Hunt, A *Brother of Miss Hunt, Elagh, Ridgeview Road, Whetstone*

Humphries, C

Ibbotson, T *Second Lieutenant, Leicester Regiment. Died 25 September 1916 age 20. Son of Walter Ibbotson, 15 Oakleigh Gardens, Whetstone. War diary records"Heavy sniping and machine gun fire at Lesboeufs, Factory Road, near Delville Wood"*

King, W *Son of Charles King, 13 Birley Road, Whetstone*

Kirby, Edward *Private, Royal Fusiliers. Died 11 November 1914 age 30. Related to either Arthur King, 3 Whetstone Place or Ernest King, Cecil Cottages Rasper Road or Sydney King, 6 North Place, Whetstone. "Took over trenches on Ypres-Menin Road. This was much the most severe shelling we have seen"*

Levy, Harold *Private, Lancashire Fusiliers. Died 10 August 1918 age 18. Vis en Artois Cemetery. Son of Jospeh Levy, 1 Guy Cliffe Cottages, Oakleigh Road, Whetstone*

Marshall, W G *Private, Queens Own Hussars. Died 23 March 1918. Noyon British Cemetery. Probably related to Allan Marshall, Ivy Bank, High Road, Whetstone*

Matthews, E *Son of Harry Matthews, 16 Bawtry Road, Whetstone*

Melhuish, Francis *Private, Gloucester Regiment. Died 23 July 1916. Thiepval Memorial. "Attack on Leipzig redoubt. The fire was so heavy that it was impossible to move"*

Newman, A *Private, Liverpool Regiment. Died of wounds 1 November 1918 age 20. Son of George Noon, 4 Oak View Terrace, Oakleigh Road, Whetstone*

Onslow, A E *Driver RFA. Died 18 October 1917 age 39. Barr Cott Cemetery*

Palmer, William *Son of Albert Plamer, 6 Sunnyside, Swan Lane, Whetstone*

Peggs, W G   *Sergeant, Bedfordhsire Regiment. Died 9 August 1916 age 23. La Neuville Cemetery, Corbie. Husband of Mrs Peggs, 1 Milverton Terrace, Totteridge Lane. "Took part in operations around Intermediate Line"*

Porter, G   *Husband of Mrs Porter, 17 Holly Terrace, Whetstone*

Proctor, A   *Private, Middlesex Regiment. Died 18 May 1917. Duisans Military Cemetery, Etrun. Son of A Proctor, Lime Cottage, High Road, Whetstone*

Price, R   *Husband of Mrs Price, 1 Hungerton Villas, Whetstone*

Ring, Melville   *Sergeant, London Regiment. Died 3 May 1915 age 28. Ypres Memorial. Husband of Mrs M Ring, Baralong, Ridgeview Road, Whetstone "Under heavy attack especially on the right. Casualties very heavy"*

Roberts, Jack   *Private, Middlesex Regiment. Died 7 October 1916. Thiepval Memorial. Son of Fred Roberts, 35 Birley Road, Whetstone. "Attack on Spectrum Trench, Casualties very heavy"*

Robins, R *(possible Raymond) Driver RFA. Died 6 December 1918 of world flu epidemic 49th Stationary Hospital. Bralo British Cemetery, Greece*

Richary, A (possibly Richards)   *Possibly son of Alfred Richards, 5 Athenaeum Road, Whetstone*

Russell, Henry   *Possibly son of Charles Russell, 4 Sunnyside, Swan Lane, Whetstone*

Rolfe, A

Smith, Frederick David   *Probably son of Frederick Smith, 18 Holly Terrace, Whetstone*

Taylor, S   *Possibly son of David Taylor, Oak Villa, Athenaeum Road, Whetstone*

Thompson, Harold E   *Rifleman, London Regiment. Died 30 October 1917 age 33. Tyne Cott Memorial. Son of Henry Thompson, 15 Sunnyside, Swan Lane, Whetstone*

Waters, H *Husband of Mrs Waters, 2 Dixon's Cottages, High Road, Whetstone*

Watts, J

Welch, Reginald *Private, 1/8 Battalion London Regiment. Died 15 November 1916 age 22. Larch Wood Cemetery. Member of old Whetstone family. "Attack on Butte de Walingcourt. 2 companies almost completely wiped out. Only 7 men survived"*

Wells, J

Williams, J *Possible son of J Williams, 7 Birley Road, Whetstone*

Williams, R

ST PAUL'S CHURCH, Woodland Road, New Southgate

ROLL OF HONOUR 1914-1919. GOD REST THEIR SOULS

Addison F G	Dolby, F G	Matthews, A T
Addison, R	Dutch, W S	Meader, A F
Ainsley, L C	Eales, E	Moles, J
Allan, L D	Edwards, H C	Moles, P J
Allan, S D	Foreman, H W	Mooney, W
Anderson, C H	Forster, W A	Nicholls, E J
Bagge, F	Foxen, T G	Panting, C E
Baker, F	Foy, A J	Parry, W H L
Baker, G	Fraser, H D	Powell, LTM
Boa, A	Gentle, C F	Rumsby, F

Bowden, J	Goldsmith, F W	Rutt, T J
Brown, G R	Grant, G L	Scarfe, A D
Brown, H J	Gurney, H T	Sexton, L A
Brown, J S	Hardie, B	Simpson, J E
Burden, C A	Harrison, R S	Simpson, W L
Burgess, J R H	Hawkes, S F	Smith, H S
Bush, A O	Heathman, J E	Smith, J T
Cameron, E	Hewlett, C H	Tingay, R
Castell, R C	Hill, F G	Tripp, H E
Clark, F W	Hunt, H	Vincent, H
Cobb, B	Johnson, A D	Walker, L F
Coleman, A E	Jones, P J	Waller, B
Coombs, H J	Jones, T W	Weedon, C
Cornell, A J H	King, P E	West, G S
Cosgrove, A W	Last, W G	Whare, F H
Cridge, A	Lawrie, R R	Wheatley, G
Cripps, A J	Leeds G	Wilkinson, J A
Crouch, E G	Lyness, L P	Woodfield, S
Day, F W	Mabbott, S C	Wooding, E G

ST PETER-LE-POER, Colney Hatch Lane

Albone, John   *Lance Corporal, Royal Fusiliers (London Regiment). Died 20 November 1917*

Allison, Henry   *Private, Royal Fusiliers (London Regiment). Died 11 November 1914*

Baker, Charles

Barks, Isaac   *Private, Middlesex Regiment. Died 23 April 1917*

Bass, John   *Private, Middlesex Regiment. Died 23 April 1917*

Batchelor, John H   *Private, Grenadier Guards. Died 5 August 1917*

Batchelor, William

Carroll, George A   *Private, 19th (Queen Alexandra's Own Royal) Hussars. Died 19 May 1917*

Clarke, Basil H   *Rifleman, London Regiment. Died 6 March 1917 age 21*

Collyer, William J

Dawkins, George F   *Private, Norfolk Regiment. Died 7 July 1918 age 21*

Defoe, Frederick   *Private, Canadian Infantry. Died 15 May 1917 age 37*

Dennis Frederick A

Ellis Thomas, W

Farrow, R

Farrow, Thomas W   *Private, Royal Fusiliers (London Regiment). Died 10 October 1916 age 25. Son of William Thomas and Ada Farrow, 14 Friern Park, North Finchley*

Farrow, Walter E

Field, H *Private, Middlesex Regiment. Died 19 August 1917*

Ford, A

Foreman, Charles *Rifleman, Rifle Brigade. Died 1 August 1917 age 19. Son of Jesse and Louise Foreman, 24 Cromwell Road, Muswell Hill*

Foxon, J

Garment, Stanley W

Gentle, Arthur G

Green, John

Goddard, John

Goddard, Owen *Sapper, Royal Engineers. Died 20 March 1917 age 35. Son of Mrs H Goddard, 31 Cromwell Road, Muswell Hill*

Harmer, Philip *Private, Hertfordshire Regiment. Died 28 March 1918 age 19. Son of George and Sarah Harmer, 1 Railway Cottages, New Southgate*

Harris, Arthur

Hawkes, Thomas

Hawkes, William *Private, Machine Gun Corps (heavy branch). Died 11 February 1917*

Hetherington, Alfred

Hooper, F

Hornibrook, Harry

Howard, George

Hudson, C

Humber, Ernest

Jackson, Cecil

James, Stanley H

Jessope, Phillip   *Private, Buffs (East Kent Regiment). Died 28 September 1915*

Kilby, William   *Private, Royal Scots Fusiliers. Died 3 April 1915*

Knight, J

Laybourne, Joseph

Lindsay, Albert   *Private, Royal Welsh Fusiliers. Died 20 July 1916*

Low, William

Marshall, William

Matthews, George

Matthews, Robert

Milsom, Ernest   *Gunner, Royal Field Artillery. Died 18 August 1918*

Mitchell, R

Mitchell, Samuel   *Private, Middlesex Regiment. Dies 21 June 1917 age 31. Son of Samuel and Fanny Mitchell, 128 Cromwell Road, Muswell Hill*

Moody, Henry

Neville, John

Newbury, Joseph

Osborne, Ernest   *Private, Royal Fusiliers (London Regiment). Died 23 March 1918*

Phillips, F

Porter, Frederick *Sergeant, Royal Fusiliers (London Regiment). Died 8 October 1918 age 29. Son of Frederick and Annie Porter, 184 Sydney Road, Muswell Hill*

Rees, Albert

Richardson, John

Richardson, Richard

Richardson, Thomas

Rook, Percy *Private, Suffolk Regiment. Died 24 April 1917 age 20. Son of Jonah and Susan Rook, 3 Shenley Cottages, Alma Road, Muswell Hill*

Rumbold, P

Sharpe, James

Smith, Arthur

Smith, George

Stagg, Sidney

Stevens, Charles

Stower, Charles A *Private, Machine Gun Corps. Died 7 May 1917*

Stower, Walter *Lance Corporal, Middlesex Regiment. Died 20 October 1916*

Tucknott, George *Private, Alexandra, Princess of Wales' Own (Yorkshire Regiment). Died 7 June 1917 age 20. Son of Rosina C Trucknott, 56 Halliwick Road, Muswell Hill*

Tyler, Walter

Upson, Charles *Sergeant, London Regiment. Died 16 September 1916*

Vaughan, John

Vidler, Bertram *Second Lieutenant, Royal Sussex Regiment. Died 12 April 1917 age 23*

Whiting, W G *Private, Middlesex Regiment. Died 7 October 1916*

Willis, Robert *Private, Middlesex Regiment. Died 19 March 1915. Son of Mrs L Willis, 8 Pembroke Road, Muswell Hill*

Wylie, Robert

APPENDIX D
ZEPPELIN RAIDS ON BRITAIN

Date	Location	Killed	Injured
1915			
19 Jan	Yarmouth	2	3
	King's Lynn	2	13
14 Apr	Tyneside	13	9
15 Apr	Essex and Suffolk	-	-
29 Apr	Suffolk	-	-
7 May	Southend	1	2
16 May	Ramsgate	2	1
26 May	Southend	3	3
31 May	**Balls Pond Road, Commercial Road, Hoxton**	**11**	**12**
3 Jun	East Riding, Essex, Kent	-	8
6 Jun	Hull, Grimsby	24	40
15 Jun	Durham, Northumberland	18	72
9 Aug	Dover, East Riding, Goole, Suffolk	17	21
12 Aug	East Sussex, Essex	6	24
17 Aug	**Leyton, Leytonstone, Wanstead**	**12**	**68**

Date	Location	Killed	Injured
7 Sep	East Suffolk	-	13
	Deptford, Isle of Dogs		
	New Cross, Rotherhithe	**18**	**25**
8 Sep	Norfolk, North Riding	4	7
	Gray's Inn Road, Holborn,		
	Liverpool Street Station	**22**	**87**
11 Sep	Essex	-	-
12 Sep	East Suffolk, Essex	-	-
13 Sep	Margate	2	6
	East Suffolk	-	-
13 Oct	Norfolk, Suffolk	8	-
	Chancery Lane, Charing Cross,		
	Farringdon Road, Limehouse,		
	Strand	**63**	**147**

1916

13 Jan	Midlands	70	128
31 Jan	Midlands, West Suffolk	70	113
5 Mar	East Riding, Hull, Kent, Leicestershire, Lincolnshire, Rutland	18	52

Date	Location	Killed	Injured
31 Mar	Essex, Lincolnshire, Suffolk	48	64
	Edinburgh	84	227
1 Apr	Durham, North Yorkshire	22	130
2 Apr	East Suffolk, Northumberland, Scotland	13	24
3 Apr	Norfolk	-	-
4 Apr	East Coast	1	9
5 Apr	County Durham, Yorkshire	1	9
25 Apr	Cambridgeshire, Lincolnshire, Norfolk, Suffolk	1	1
26 Apr	East Suffolk, Essex, Kent	-	1
27 Apr	Kent	-	-
1 May	East Coast, Scotland	-	-
2 May	Northumberland, Yorkshire, Scotland	9	30
28 Jul	Lincolnshire, Norfolk	-	-
31 Jul	Cambridgeshire, Kent, Lincolnshire, Norfolk, Suffolk	-	-
3 Aug	East Suffolk, Kent, Norfolk	-	-

Date	Location	Killed	Injured
9 Aug	Norfolk, Northern Counties	10	16
23 Aug	East Suffolk	-	-
24 Aug	**West Ferry Road**	**9**	**40**
25 Aug	East Coast	-	-
2 Sep	**Blackheath, Plumstead**	**3**	**14**
23 Sep	Kent, Lincolnshire, Norfolk	18	130
	Brixton, Kennington, Streatham	**22**	**75**
25 Sep	Lancashire, Lincolnshire, Yorkshire	43	31
1 Oct	Hertfordshire, Home Counties, Midlands	1	1
27 Nov	Cheshire, Durham, Staffordshire, Yorkshire	4	37

1917

Date	Location	Killed	Injured
16 Mar	Kent, Sussex	-	-
23 May	Essex, Norfolk, Suffolk	3	16
17 Jun	Kent, Suffolk	3	16
21 Aug	East Yorkshire	-	1
19 Oct	Eastern Counties, Midlands	4	7
	Camberwell, Hither Green, Piccadilly	**32**	**48**

Date	Location	Killed	Injured
1918			
12 Mar	East Riding, Hull	1	-
13 Mar	Durham, Hartlepool	8	39
14 Apr	Lancashire, Lincoln, Warwick	7	20
	London	**181**	**504**
	Rest of Britain	**541**	**1311**
	Total	**722**	**1815**

Estimated damage to property

London	**£1,000,000**
Rest of Britain	**£500,000**

APPENDIX E
AEROPLANE RAIDS ON BRITAIN

Date	Location	Killed	Injured
1914			
21 Dec	Seaplane raid on Dover	-	-
24 Dec	Seaplane raid on Dover	-	-
25 Dec	Seaplane raid on Dover	-	-
1915			
11 Feb	Colchester, Essex	-	-
16 Apr	Faversham, Sittingbourne	-	-
4 Jul	East Suffolk	-	-
13 Sep	Margate	2	6
1916			
22 Jan	Dover	1	6
23 Jan	Kent	-	-
9 Feb	Broadstairs, Margate	-	3
20 Feb	East Suffolk, Kent	1	1
1 Mar	Broadstairs, Margate	1	-

Date	Location	Killed	Injured
19 Mar	Seaplane raid on Deal, Dover, Margate, Ramsgate	14	26
25 Apr	Dover	-	-
3 May	Deal	-	3
19 May	Dover, Kent	1	2
9 Jul	Dover, North Foreland	-	-
12 Aug	Seaplane raid on Dover	-	7
22 Sep	Dover, Kent	-	-
22 Oct	Sheerness	-	2
23 Oct	Margate	-	-

1917

25 Feb	Broadstairs, Margate	3	1
1 Mar	Kent	-	6
16 Mar	Westgate	-	-
17 Mar	Kent	-	6
5 Apr	Kent, Ramsgate	-	-
7 May	**Hackney, Holloway**	**1**	**2**
24 May	Folkestone	95	195

Date	Location	Killed	Injured
5 Jun	Medway, Thames Estuary	13	24
13 Jun	Essex, Margate	77	106
	Barking, East Ham, Fenchurch Street, Liverpool Street, Poplar Royal Albert Docks	**162**	**426**
17 Jun	**London**	**158**	**425**
4 Jul	Harwich, Suffolk	17	30
7 Jul	Margate	-	-
	Chingford, Edmonton, Stoke Newington, Tottenham, Tower Hill	**54**	**190**
22 Jul	Essex, Suffolk	13	26
12 Aug	Essex, Margate	32	46
22 Aug	Dover, Margate, Ramsgate	12	25
2 Sep	Dover	1	6
3 Sep	Sheerness	132	96
4 Sep	**London**, South east counties	19	71
24 Sep	Essex, Kent, **London**	21	70
25 Sep	**South east London**	**9**	**23**
28 Sep	Home Counties	-	-

Date	Location	Killed	Injured
29 Sep	**Chiswick, Dalston, Holloway, Notting Hill, Waterloo**	13	86
30 Sep	**London**	14	38
1 Oct	Essex, Kent, **London**	11	41
31 Oct	Dover, Kent	-	-
	Charlton, Greenwich, Isle of Dogs, Streatham, Tooting	5	2
6 Dec	Essex, Kent	6	21
	Dulwich, Stockwell *(1st Gotha raid)*	2	7
18 Dec	**Bermondsey, Hackney, Kentish Town King's Cross, Westminster, Walworth**	13	79

1918

28 Jan	**Bethnal Green, Camden Town, Holborn, King's Cross, London Bridge, Whitechapel**	65	159
29 Jan	**Brentford, Kew, Richmond, Wanstead**	10	10

Date	Location	Killed	Injured
16 Feb	Beckenham, Chelsea, Woolwich	12	2
17 Feb	Camberwell, King's Cross, Lewisham	21	32
19 Feb	Essex, Kent, London	-	-
7 Mar	Clapham, Hampstead, St John's Wood	23	39
19 May	Bethnal Green, Camberwell, Catford, Islington, Kentish Town, Lewisham, Poplar, Stratford	48	172
17 Jun	Kent	-	-
18 Jul	Kent	-	-
20 Jul	Kent	-	-
	London	487	1434
	Rest of Britain	472	833
	Total	959	2267

Estimated damage to property

London £1,019,000

APPENDIX F
PENSIONS FOR THE WAR DISABLED

In 1918 pensions were the responsibility of the newly created Ministry of Pensions where a staff of 527 men and 8195 women attempted to deal with the huge number of claimants. According to *Hansard* there were between 15,000 and 20,000 new cases each week. Pensions were paid through Post Offices where extra staff was also employed. In January 1919 the numbers receiving pensions were:

Disabled Officers	10,212
Disabled Nurses	383
Disabled Men	525,862
Widows of Officers	8,580
Widows of Men	179, 273
Children of Deceased Officers	9,213
Children of Deceased Men	339,829
Children of Disabled Men	490,010
Officers' Other Dependants	3,481
Men's Other Dependents	214,004

The causes of disability were:

Eyesight cases	13,736
Amputated legs	15,447

Amputated arms	7,342
Wounds or injuries to legs	70,067
Wounds to arms	49,226
Wounds to hands	23,826
Wounds to head or face	20,805
Hernia	4,577
Miscellaneous wounds	25,846
Chest complaints and gassing	57,858
Nerves, including shell shock	29,696
Insanity	4,423
Deafness	9,067
Frost bite	3,723
Miscellaneous	194,799

Hansard noted that men recovered from injuries more quickly than from illnesses.

St Dunstan's trained blind soldiers and discharged 46 during 1918.

27,437 men were fitted with artificial limbs in the first 8 months of 1919 with a further 27,436 on the waiting lists. For limbless men, 608 tricycles were supplied up to 31 December 1918. The number discharged from medical treatment up to December 1918 was 92,500. On Christmas Day 1918 42,428 men were under hospital treatment.

Under the Royal Warrant of 1918 the UK war disability pension was £71 10s 0d per year (£3102 at today's prices) with £17 10s 0d for the first child and £10 10s 0d for any subsequent child. In June 1919 a further 20% was added. The widows' pension was £35 rising to £39 at age £45.

By comparison, in France the annual pension was £48, in Italy it was £30 with £12 for a wife. In the USA a married man received £112 and in Germany the pension was £36 to £65 depending on the nature of the disability.